TEXAS CATALOG
HISTORIC AMERICAN BUILDINGS SURVEY

TEXAS CATALOG

HISTORIC AMERICAN BUILDINGS SURVEY

Office of Archeology and Historic Preservation

National Park Service • Department of the Interior

COMPILED BY PAUL GOELDNER

Edited by Lucy Pope Wheeler and S. Allen Chambers, Jr.

A List of Measured Drawings, Photographs and Written Documentation in the Survey—1974

TRINITY UNIVERSITY PRESS • SAN ANTONIO, TEXAS

The Trinity University Press gratefully acknowledges the assistance of Exxon Company, U.S.A. in making this book possible.

Front cover: House of the Seasons, Jefferson

Back cover: Colonel Walter Gresham House, Galveston

Library of Congress Card Catalog Number 75-28599
Printed in the United States of America
Printed by Best Printing Company
SBN # 911536-62-0

THE HISTORIC AMERICAN BUILDINGS SURVEY

The Historic American Buildings Survey (HABS) is a long range program to assemble a national archives of historic American architecture. Begun in 1933 as a Works Progress Administration (WPA) project, the Survey represented the Federal government's first major step toward the cataloging and preservation of historic structures. The initial phases of the Survey were so successful that within two years of its inception, a tripartite agreement was signed among the National Park Service, the Library of Congress, and the American Institute of Architects to establish the program on a permanent basis. This agreement, with some subsequent modifications, remains the operating structure of HABS. The active recording program of the Historic American Buildings Survey was terminated at the outbreak of World War II, but recognition of the continuing value of the program led to its reactivation in 1957, and extensive recording has gone on since that time. In 1967, the Survey became a part of the Division of Historic Architecture of the Office of Archeology and Historic Preservation, where it operates in cooperation with the other historic preservation programs of the National Park Service. John C. Poppeliers is currently (1974) the Chief of the Survey. Under the tripartite agreement, HABS administers the program and is responsible for qualitative standards, organization of projects, and selection of subjects for recording. The Library of Congress is the depository for the records which are serviced by the staff of the Prints and Photographs Division. The American Institute of Architects provides professional counsel through its national membership.

The Survey intends to provide a thorough and accurate picture of the builder's art throughout the United States by including as many construction types, use types, and styles as possible. Structures represented in the Survey span the period from both prehistoric and colonial times to early twentieth century and include examples from all 50 states, the District of Columbia, Puerto Rico, and the Virgin Islands. Today, the Survey's records are produced primarily through annual measured drawing projects which employ student architects and university faculty supervisors during the summer recess. The collection now includes approximately 16,000 buildings represented by about 31,000 drawings, 47,000 photographs, and 23,500 pages of written data. The Survey's goal is the broadest possible coverage for all areas, periods, styles, and types of American architecture.

Those who are interested in consulting the records of the Survey may either visit the Division of Prints and Photographs, Library of Congress, or consult the catalogs that have been published by the Survey. A comprehensive, geographically arranged *Catalog* was published in 1941; a *Supplement* appeared in 1959. More recently, because of the extensiveness of HABS holdings, new catalogs are being published by states and areas. To date, state catalogs have appeared for New Hampshire, Maine, Massachusetts, Wisconsin, Chicago and nearby Illinois Areas, Michigan, the District of Columbia, and Utah. Catalogs for New Jersey, Rhode Island, Philadelphia, South Carolina, Indiana, Ohio, and Virginia are currently in progress. Most of these publications can be consulted in major university or public libraries. Further questions regarding the consultation of records and ordering of reproductions may be addressed to:

> Division of Prints and Photographs
> Library of Congress
> Washington, D.C. 20450

Questions regarding HABS recording and publishing programs may be addressed to:

> Historic American Buildings Survey
> National Park Service
> Washington, D.C. 20240

Recently, the National Park Service published *Recording Historic Buildings*, compiled by Professor Harley J. McKee. Based on the Survey's long experience, this volume is a pioneering effort which establishes standards for the gathering of both historic and architectural documentation. Already it is widely regarded as the definitive work in the field. Copies may be purchased from:

> Superintendent of Documents
> U.S. Printing Office
> Washington, D.C. 20402

CONTENTS

TEXAS ARCHITECTURE AND HABS RECORDING
IN TEXAS: AN OUTLINE

"Diversity" best describes the terrain, the climate, the history, the people, and the architecture of Texas. Communities along the Rio Grande were outposts of Spanish civilization before 1700, while counties on the high plains which are today among the State's most populous were almost uninhabited until after 1900. Dwellings along the coast often have double galleries to catch the cooling breeze while dugouts help protect against the harsh winds of the Panhandle. In the Lone Star State, there is no single thread of architectural development easily traced from its beginning, as is done with some validity in the states of the Eastern seaboard.

The pages that follow attempt to describe and illustrate examples of the great diversity that is so apparent in the history of the art of building in Texas. Along with the outline of the story of Texas architecture runs the story of the efforts made by the Historic American Buildings Survey to record these examples, from its inception in the years of the Depression to the present.

On December 12, 1933, the National Park Service issued Circular No. 1 of the Historic American Buildings Survey. While the Bulletin stated that there was an obvious need to document "important architectural specimens which remain from the old days" so that they "should not pass into unrecorded oblivion," there was another reason for initiating the Survey at this particular time. This was stated in the forthright subtitle of the circular: "A Ten Weeks Unemployment Relief Project for One Thousand Architects and Architectural Draftsmen."

To administer this vast recording project, which actually began one month later, the country was divided into thirty-nine districts, each under the supervision of a District Officer. These officers were nominated by the American Institute of Architects and appointed by the Secretary of the Interior. Texas was District 33, and its capable District Officer was Marvin Eickenroht, F.A.I.A., of San Antonio. For 35 years, until his death in February 1969, Mr. Eickenroht was intimately connected with HABS activities in Texas.

District 33 was allocated forty men to accomplish the stated task of recording the historic buildings of Texas. Field teams were organized into squads of two, four, or six men, depending on the size of the project. The ranking member of the group was designated the squad leader and was directly responsible to the District Officer.

The initial phase of HABS recording, which was funded by the Civil Works Administration (CWA), lasted only three months—from January to March, 1934. In this short time, a tremendous amount of work was accomplished. Nationally, the Sur-

Mission Concepción, San Antonio/Arthur Stewart, Photo 1936

vey teams drew 5,110 sheets of measured drawings and took 3,260 photographs of 882 structures. The Texas teams produced some 177 sheets of measured drawings and 242 photographs during this 1934 effort. These earliest HABS Texas records well reflect the diversity and richness of style, type, and national origin of the State's architectural heritage.

Mission San José, San Antonio/Arthur Stewart, Photo 1936

Perhaps the most extensive records made at this time were the measured drawings of the Spanish Missions of San Antonio. These mission churches and their related structures are among the most treasured buildings in the State, and rightly so. The vaults and dome of Concepción (TEX-319) have survived from 1752 to demonstrate the sophisticated construction techniques of the missionary architects. The square twin towers complete a typical church facade which no longer exists or was never realized at the other missions.

More restoration has been necessary at San José (TEX-333), where the Indian dwellings in the extensive ramparts and the buttressed granary provide a clearer understanding of the totality of a mission community. The rich stone carving of the church facade and the "rose window" are beautiful examples of Spanish colonial architectural ornament and justify the epithet "Queen of the Missions."

Espada (TEX-320) and San Juan Capistrano (TEX-321) never attained their projected size due to a decline in Indian population and withdrawal of governmental protection before they reached completion. However, their chapels each have interesting facades projecting above the roofs in baroque outlines and pierced by belfry arches. Parts of the acequias which provided irrigation water to the missions' fields are still in use; the Espada aqueduct is a pair of arches which are a modest reminder of its imperial Roman antecedents.

Another important group of "ethnic" structures recorded by HABS in 1934 were buildings erected by German settlers, who constituted the largest and best organized group of nineteenth-century immigrants to Texas. The towns of Fredericksburg and New Braunfels were almost entirely German, and the Teutonic element was also significant throughout a large area between Galveston and San Antonio.

Many German farms around Fredericksburg were remote from town in comparison with European village precedent familiar to the settlers. To enjoy the life of the community it became customary to build Sunday houses in Fredericksburg to provide for the needs of the farmers' families when they came into town for a weekend of shopping, socializing and church-going. One of the most attractive and representative of these is the Staudt Sunday House (TEX-33-A-8). Generally, they had only one room on the ground floor, with a loft above which was reached by an exterior stair.

While native limestone is the predominant building material in Fredericksburg, half-timber or "fachwerk" structures are quite numerous around New Braunfels. Until restoration the half-timbering of the Ferdinand Lindheimer House (TEX-374) was concealed by weatherboarding. HABS records, made both in the 1930's and in 1972, show the house in both phases.

Prominent among nineteenth-century colonizers in Texas was Henry Castro, who established the towns of Castroville, Quihi, and D'Hanis on a grant west of San Antonio. Alsatians formed the nucleus of the Castro colony but it was multinational.

Following a traditional pattern, several Castroville buildings combined a family's business and residence. Among these were the houses of Laurent Quintle (TEX-362), Joseph Carlé (TEX-390), and Gerhard Ihnken (TEX-365), all of which had second-story porches or balconies.

Ferdinand Lindheimer House, New Braunfels/Roy Pledger, Photo 1972

Joseph Carlé House and Store, Castroville/Arthur Stewart, Photo 1936

Gerhard Ihnken House, Castroville, Detail of Buttress/
Richard MacAllister, Photo 1936

Quihi's Louis Boehle House (TEX-33-A-18) represents a rare American example of stable and residence in the same structure. Unfortunately, little remains of this charmingly irregular design. Attempts of French Utopian socialists to establish an Icarian Colony in Denton County were disastrous and La Reunion, a similar experiment near Dallas, was also short-lived, but French influence in the young cities of Texas has endured. At Austin the French Legation (TEX-33-C-1), occupied briefly by Count Alphonse de Saligny, is among the few reminders of a decade when Texas was an independent nation pursuing its own diplomatic objectives. Casement windows and a dormered hip roof may be regarded as French characteristics, but the wood construction is all-American.

French Legation, Austin/Jack E. Boucher, Photo 1966

Panna Maria, founded in 1854, is said to be the oldest Polish Catholic community in America. The Polish farm families who now live in northern Karnes County are frequently descendants of the original settlers on the land. Few of the original houses remain, but HABS records from the 1930's show the Moczygamba (TEX-312) and Pawelek (TEX-314) houses to be like the stone and stucco houses of German settlers in having attic spaces accessible only by exterior stairs or ladders. The uniquely Polish characteristic was the application of rich colors to the stucco and plaster surfaces.

Of course, not all of the HABS records produced in 1934 were of building types so obviously reflective of European precedent. Many more indigenous American types were also recorded, as well as types brought to Texas by settlers from the Eastern states.

"Sebastopol" (TEX-33-A-9) in Seguin is one of the former. Seguin, described in 1857 by Frederick Law Olmsted in his *A Journey through Texas* as "the prettiest town in Texas," contains a number of concrete buildings. Olmsted noted that these buildings had "thick walls of gravel and lime, raised a foot at a time, between boards, which hold the mass in place until it is solidified." Although Olmsted says the materials were used as dug at the site, local historians attribute the durability of the natural concrete to a formula or additive of Dr. Richard Parks, a Seguin chemist. "Sebastopol" is innovative in having a rooftop reservoir concealed by a broad fascia. This provided cooling as well as a water supply.

Liendo (TEX-33-B-4), near Hempstead, is an example of a Texas Plantation House recorded during the first years of the Survey. Built in 1853 as the plantation home of Leonard Croce, the Greek Revival structure is reflective of types built in older sections of the South.

The cessation of recording under the CWA program in March 1934 was abrupt in some instances. Point Isabel Lighthouse (TEX-33-Ab-1), measured and photographed in 1934, was not drawn until 1936. Because of the amount of such unfinished business, but due in far greater measure to the success of the first phase of HABS recording, a number of states decided to continue the program with state, rather than Federal, relief

8

funds. In order to coordinate all these state efforts and to make sure the uniformity and high standards that had been initially established were continued, the National Park Service, the American Institute of Architects, and the Library of Congress in June 1934 signed an agreement to establish HABS as the official national program for the collection and disposition of historic American architectural records.

One provision of this agreement was that the country was redistricted to conform with the sixty-seven chapters of the A.I.A. then existing. Accordingly, by late 1934, Texas had been divided into three districts: North Texas, whose District Officer was Otto M. Lang of Dallas; South Texas, whose District Officer was Birdsall P. Briscoe of Houston; and West Texas, under the leadership of Mr. Eickenroht, with able assistance from Bartlett Cocke, Deputy District Officer. In addition, Mr. Eickenroht was appointed Division Officer of the Southern Division, in which Texas was placed. This was one of four National Divisions made at this time.

In January 1936 Federal funding was again made available for the HABS program, this time under the Works Progress Administration (WPA). This funding continued until the outbreak of World War II, when all Depression projects came to an end. When the first complete catalog of the HABS collection was published in 1941, it listed 272 structures which had been recorded in Texas. Because the men available to do the work during this first period of recording were professional architects, great emphasis was placed upon recording buildings by means of measured drawings. Photographs and data—historical as well as architectural—received less attention.

While some effort during this second phase of HABS recording was devoted to obtaining additional or supplementary records on buildings which had already been covered, the major emphasis was on heretofore neglected areas and types. Consequently, log houses, forts, ranch buildings, inns, etc., joined the Spanish missions and Greek Revival mansions already included. Perhaps not so dramatic, visually impressive, or in as sound condition as some of the major monuments, they are an integral part of the architectural history and development of the State.

With few possessions and minimal tools, Texas' pioneer settlers followed a pattern familiar in other states, building their first houses of materials available at the site, log or adobe. Such crude shelter was usually regarded as temporary, but some examples have proven very durable.

Among the earliest log houses was the Gaines-McGowan House (TEX-267) at the place where the Spanish "Camino Real" crossed the Sabine River, near present-day Milam. Its dog-trot plan is sometimes described as a three-room plan with the middle room left out, or two one-room cabins with one connecting roof. The open central space became a standard feature of the Texas house because it permitted cool breezes to circulate.

Along the Rio Grande the pioneers were ranchers whose building techniques were those of Mexico. The Treviño House (TEX-3112) at San Ygnacio is an example of a ranch headquarters begun in 1851 with a few rooms and elaborated over a period of twenty years. Sandstone walls are plastered with adobe and the nearly flat roofs were originally of native concrete supported on wooden beams. The central courtyard plan has its origins in Mediterranean antiquity and was also used in the ranch fort of Ben Leaton (TEX-3103) near Presidio.

Fort McKavett/Arthur Stewart, Photo 1936

Near Shafter, Milton Faver used adobe block to build the Fortin de Cienega (TEX-3119), a square stockade with two defense towers at opposite corners and a row of flat-roofed rooms inside the south and west perimeter. This cattle ranch headquarters was built in the late 1850's.

In the last decades of Indian warfare the United States Army established lines of defense to protect trade routes and pioneer settlement. The forts constructed by the army were not fortified enclosures, but posts from which units could make scouting expeditions. Two of the best examples are Fort Davis (TEX-3102) and Fort McKavett (TEX-3111), both photographed by HABS in 1936. These forts were established in the early 1850's, abandoned during the Civil War, reactivated and rebuilt more permanently after 1867. The rapid advance of the frontier made all of the Texas forts only briefly active as outposts and both Fort McKavett and Fort Davis were principally used as convalescent centers, valued for their healthful climates, in the years preceding their deactivation in 1883 and 1891, respectively.

East Texas has numerous examples of antebellum plantation houses which were recorded by HABS in 1936. Among these impressive reminders of the past are Cedar Hall (TEX-225) near Plantersville; the Colonel John Dewberry Plantation House (TEX-133) west of Bullard; and the A. Wiley Hill House (TEX-336) south of Bastrop. All of these were built in the decade preceding the Civil War and recorded by HABS in the 1930's.

In Brazoria County, remains at Chenango Plantation (TEX-283), near Angleton, depict more unsavory aspects of the slave economy. A sugar mill and slave quarters were part of this huge plantation established in the 1830's. It was also a depot for smuggling slaves from the West Indies.

Probably the most complete of the State's antebellum plantation complexes is that of E. Sterling C. Robertson (TEX-394) at Salado, where the slave quarters are a long one-story stone building and the main house a two-story frame structure with porches. Unlike the usual projecting pedimented porticoes, the front and rear porches of the Robertson house are recessed into a hip-roofed block. HABS records include the entire complex.

In its original state, the plantation house of Colonel William Madison Sledge (TEX-25) near Chappell Hill was an interpretation of a Palladian villa with its principal rooms on the upper floor or "piano nobile," which was constructed of wood with porticoes at north and south. The lower, service level of brick is the only portion which has survived extensive remodeling.

William Garrett's Plantation House (TEX-33-D-2), west of San Augustine, is interesting as an expanded version of the earliest Texas cabins. Its central hall is an elaboration of the dog-trot and its porch along the south front is absorbed into the gabled mass with chimneys at each end. Only the dormers required by the second floor break the outlines of the typical Texas house form.

William Garrett Plantation House, San Augustine Vicinity/
F. O. Taylor, Photo 1934

Almost nothing is typically Texan in the house built near Washington by John M. Brown (TEX-213), a planter from South Carolina. Its elegant proportions are ornamented with mouldings said to have been imported from New York.

Some planters chose to live in towns rather than on their plantations. One, Dr. Charles W. Tait, built a great house in Columbus (TEX-282) to remove his family from the unhealthful lowlands along the Colorado River.

From World War II to the mid-1950's no active HABS recording projects were undertaken. Records dating from this period were obtained primarily as donations from individuals or organizations. By 1957, when the Historic American Buildings Survey was reinstituted nationally as an active recording program, two important innovations were incorporated.

Unlike the early HABS program, in which practicing architects were employed to produce its records, post-war recording largely relies on summer field teams of student architects under the direct supervision of university professors of architecture. In addition to providing new material for the Survey's collection, this procedure also affords invaluable training and experience to future architects and architectural historians. The major portion of the HABS records continues to be produced in this manner. Summer projects are now normally financed on a matching fund basis in cooperation with state or local governmental units and private organizations.

The second innovation of the 1950's was the introduction of the HABS Inventory form (HABSI), a one-page outline devised to accommodate succinct and pertinent information on interesting buildings and to aid in the establishment of priorities for possible future full-scale recording with measured drawings, photographs, and data. The HABSI forms were filled out and donated by architects, historians, and historical groups in the State. With the expansion of the National Register of Historic Places after the passage of the National Historic Preservation Act of 1966, the responsibility for this type of recording was assumed by the states and was gradually phased out by HABS. A listing of the Texas buildings recorded on these Inventory forms appears at the end of this catalog.

In 1959, two years after the reactivation of HABS, a Catalog supplement was issued to list the records obtained since the 1941 Catalog. Texas, however, is not represented in that Catalog, and it was not until the next decade that recording in the State picked up the momentum it had formerly enjoyed, a momentum that today shows no signs of diminishing.

Among the first Texas records of the 1960's were those done in Roma by and under the direction of W. Eugene George. Roma was the head of navigation on the Rio Grande. It attained a

Church of Our Lady of Refuge of Sinners, Roma/
W. Eugene George, Photo 1961

measure of distinction in 1854 when the Church of Our Lady of
Refuge of Sinners (TEX-3135) was built from a design of Father
Pierre Keralum, a missionary priest with an architectural educa-
tion. In the 1880's the commercial importance of Roma justified
several elaborately detailed brick structures designed and built
by Heinrich Portscheller, who also worked in nearby Rio Grande
City. Portscheller came to Texas after deserting Maximilian's
army in Mexico. A building like the Nestor Saéns store (TEX-
3129) shows how sympathetically he served his clients; his style
nowhere suggests his German origins.

Another early accomplishment of the revived HABS program
was the production of seventeen sheets of measured drawings on
San Antonio's Mission San Antonio de Valero, known to all the
world as "The Alamo" (TEX-318). HABS recording of this major
Texas building had long been urged by Dr. Ernest Allen Connally
and was carried out in 1961 by students at the University of
Texas. The mission, established in 1718, was relocated on the east
bank of the San Antonio River in 1724. Its chapel, begun about
twenty years later, was probably never completed but the arched

14

The Alamo, San Antonio/Jack E. Boucher, Photo 1961

entrance in a composition of niches and attached columns is a lasting achievement of stone carving, the familiar facade of the Alamo.

After secularization in 1794 the mission complex saw misuse and disuse in the years before the Texas Revolution. In 1835 Mexican General Cos turned the Alamo into a fort, pulling down the arches of the already roofless church to build an inclined plane for his cannon. Although Cos was defeated by Texas forces, a superior Mexican army under Santa Anna returned in February 1836 to besiege a band of 187 Texans in the Alamo. These, including Bonham, Bowie, Crockett and Travis, were killed on March 6. Their martyrdom in the cause for Texas independence has made the Alamo perhaps the most revered and familiar building in Texas.

The first full-scale summer recording project in Texas was that carried out in Jefferson in 1966. River navigation made Jefferson the gateway to northeast Texas, but the railroads by-passed it and its stagnation contributed to the preservation of its finest architecture. The Jefferson HABS team was comprised of

Willard B. Robinson, A.I.A., of Texas Tech University, who was the supervisor, and four student architects. In addition to sixteen structures in Jefferson, this team also recorded the Andrews-Taylor House in neighboring Harrison County. Besides its intrinsic architectural merit, this building has significance as the childhood home of Mrs. Lyndon Johnson.

Among the local contributors and cooperators insuring the success of the Jefferson project were the Dan Lester Drilling Company, the Excelsior Hotel, Mrs. A. K. Payne, the Jessie Allen Wise Garden Club, and the Marion County Chamber of Commerce. One of the buildings recorded was the "House of the Seasons" (TEX-142), designed for Benjamin H. Epperson and built c. 1872. It is a rare example of the Italianate mode in Texas. Its square cupola is glazed on each side with a different color to represent the four seasons and the light filters to the floors below through the oculus of a miniature dome.

House of the Seasons, Jefferson/Jack E. Boucher, Photo 1966

House of the Seasons/Jack E. Boucher, Photo 1966

Jefferson Courthouse, Jefferson/Harry Starnes, Photo 1936

Also recorded in 1966 was the Texas State Capitol (TEX-3326), a structure that had hitherto been "untouched" by HABS because its date (1882) was later than those given preference for recording by the Survey in its earliest days. The Capitol's architect, Elijah E. Myers, was selected in an anonymous competition. He was America's most prolific designer of public buildings, having designed many city halls and courthouses and three statehouses. Texas pink granite is the principal wall construction material of this impressive building.

Texas State Capitol/Jack E. Boucher, Photo 1966

Texas State Capitol/Jack E. Boucher, Photo 1966

Texas State Capitol/Jack E. Boucher, Photo 1966

Texas State Capitol/Jack E. Boucher, Photo 1966

The Jefferson summer project was followed in 1967 by a similar endeavor in Galveston. When Galveston was Texas' principal port, its flourishing commerce built a city of concentrated elegance. Several grand mansions were produced in the decade before the Civil War. The grandest was probably that of James Mareau Brown (TEX-33-B-3), a three-story brick palace with broad, bracketed overhangs and a two-deck veranda of cast iron lace. The interiors are equally spacious and ornate with generous use of carved walnut, moulded plaster, fresco, mirrors, and gold leaf.

Probably the finest Greek Revival public building in Texas is that built by the Federal government as a custom house, post office, and courthouse (TEX-259) at Galveston. The proportions and detailing suggest the work of a professional architect but the drawings prepared in 1856 by Ammi B. Young, Supervising Architect of the U.S. Treasury, were definitely not those used for constructing the building. The Ionic and Corinthian colonnades are crisply detailed in cast iron.

A second period of mansion building in Galveston coincides with the dates of the Colonel Walter Gresham house (TEX-2103), 1887–1893. Popularly known as the Bishop's Palace from its later use as the residence of the Roman Catholic Diocese of Galveston, this design of Nicholas Clayton demonstrates the complex silhouette of chimneys, turrets and dormers characteristic of the era. Stained glass, marble, tapestries, oak, and curly walnut contribute to the overwhelmingly ornate interior and to the house's well-deserved fame as one of the State's best-known examples of late nineteenth-century architecture.

In Galveston, elegance invaded the marketplace more than in other Texas cities. There are fine earlier examples, but the Trueheart-Adriance Building (TEX-291), also designed by Nicholas Clayton and built in 1881, is representative of the decorative possibilities of cast iron and polychrome masonry.

By the time the 1967 recording team began its work in Galveston, an impressive foundation had been laid. In June 1966 the Galveston Historical Foundation voted to launch a multi-staged program to inventory and survey the island city's historic architecture. Under the able direction of John C. Garner, Jr., the island was first canvassed and some 1,000 structures of interest were noted. HABS Inventory forms were then prepared on many of these. These forms were reviewed in turn and HABS photo-data books with full architectural and historical data were next prepared on twenty-five of the most noteworthy buildings.

Then, as the last stage, the Historic American Buildings Survey team began its work in the summer of 1967. Narrowing the number of buildings from the previous stage, the summer team produced measured drawings on nine buildings. Supervisor of the project was Professor Melvin M. Rotsch, Texas A & M University. He was assisted by four student architects.

As in Jefferson, the citizens of Galveston responded munificently to the project. The Galveston Historical Foundation, which organized the project and acted as the local cooperating agency with HABS, received generous assistance from the Moody Foundation, the Harris and Eliza Kempner Fund, and numerous individuals.

James Mareau Brown House, Galveston/Harry L. Starnes, Photo 1936

Trueheart-Adriance Building, Galveston/Allen Stross, Photo 1967

John C. Trube House, Galveston/Allen Stross, Photo 1967

Galveston Bagging and Cordage Company, Galveston/
Allen Stross, Photo 1967

U. S. Custom House, Galveston/Allen Stross, Photo 1967

St. Mary's Cathedral, Galveston/Allen Stross, Photo 1967

Morris Lasker House, Galveston/Allen Stross, Photo 1967

Gresham House, Galveston/Allen Stross, Photo 1967

While records were still being completed on the Galveston project, a similar undertaking was being launched in San Antonio and Bexar County. San Antonio's history is longer and more varied than that of any other Texas city. While HABS had obtained records on its famous missions in 1934 and 1936, it now concentrated on some of the later structures, in addition to obtaining further material on the earlier buildings.

Beginning in the fall of 1967, Mr. Garner, on "loan" from the Galveston Historical Foundation to the San Antonio Conservation Society, set up a survey patterned after Galveston's. Again, an initial checklist was prepared, and from this HABS Inventory forms were made on eighty-seven buildings. Complete HABS photo-data books were then prepared for thirty-six buildings and seven building groups or complexes. Then, as the final thrust of this project, a HABS team arrived in June 1968 to make measured drawings of seventeen of these buildings. The team, under the supervision of Professor Wesley I. Shank of Iowa State University, consisted of four student architects. Among the buildings and building groups recorded were the Ursuline Academy (TEX-32), the United States Arsenal Depot Complex (TEX-3188), and the Bexar County Courthouse (TEX-3174).

With the departure of Spanish and Mexican clergy after the Texas Revolution, the Catholic Church in Texas was revived by appointment of a French bishop. French-speaking Ursuline nuns came from New Orleans to San Antonio. Their first academic building was a two-story, galleried design of stuccoed pisé-de-terre, a construction technique which was a specialty of Jules Poinsard, architect and builder. It was erected in 1851. Both it and later additions to the complex were recorded.

The U.S. Arsenal records consist of drawings, data, and photographs of a complex begun in 1859 and used as an arsenal until 1947. In all, six buildings, including the Commanding Officer's Quarters, the magazine, and stables, were recorded here.

In the decade of the 1890's J. Riely Gordon of San Antonio was Texas' most prolific courthouse architect. The Bexar County Courthouse is a superb example of his early work and shows his indebtedness to H. H. Richardson.

Ursuline Academy, San Antonio/Dewey G. Mears, Photo 1968

Ursuline Convent, San Antonio/Dewey G. Mears, Photo 1968

The San Antonio project was a mutual effort of HABS, the San Antonio Conservation Society, and the Bexar County Historical Survey Committee. In addition, the San Antonio Chapter of the American Institute of Architects gave guidance and advice.

Beginning in 1971, HABS has been the fortunate recipient of a number of measured drawings of Texas ranch structures and related buildings which were measured and drawn, removed from their original sites, and reassembled on the grounds of Texas Tech University at Lubbock, where they form a living museum of ranching history called "The Ranch Headquarters." Instigated by Jerry L. Rogers, then its Director, these drawings, whose first purpose was to insure that the reconstructions be as accurate as possible, were done in the standard HABS format and donated to the Survey. Willard B. Robinson supervised the Texas Tech students who prepared the drawings. These records are of such diverse building types as a saddle-and-harness house, a dugout and a bunkhouse. They make up a unique group of structures which HABS is fortunate to be able to include in its records.

In 1969 W. Eugene George, who had already done so much for the preservation and recording of historic Texas buildings as Dean of the College of Architecture, University of Houston, and as the A.I.A. State Preservation Officer, suggested to the Survey the possibility of a recording project in the Texas German settlements in Comal and Fayette Counties under the auspices of the "Texas Pioneer Arts Foundation." This project came to fruition in the summer of 1972, when a contract agreement was entered into between Professor Melvin M. Rotsch and HABS to record these buildings. On Professor Rotsch's team were Professor Roy C. Pledger of Texas A & M University and two student architects. One or two of the nine structures recorded at this time had also been photographed in the 1930's, and a comparison between the records reveals many changes. As an example, Round Top's Bethlehem Lutheran Church (TEX-3124) was recorded both in 1936 and 1972. The 1936 photographs show a rather neglected, ill-kept rural church, while the later ones reveal the care and attention now given to this significant structure.

Bethlehem Lutheran Church, Round Top/Harry Starnes, Photo 1936

31

Bethlehem Lutheran Church/Roy Pledger, Photo 1972

Another recent contribution to the Collection was the 1972 donation of a set of measured drawings of the Pollock-Capps House (TEX-3240) in Fort Worth. These were done at the University of Texas at Arlington under the direction of Associate Professor J. Daniel Spears. Other than a Morehead-Gano Log House (TEX-3269), the records on which were also a donation, this building is the only one in the Dallas-Fort Worth area currently represented in the Collection. However, several buildings in the area have been recorded on HABS Inventory forms.

Professor Rotsch was again involved in a major Texas recording project in the summer of 1973. Thanks to the efforts of Mr. Wayne Bell, the Historic Sites and Restoration Branch of the Texas Parks and Wildlife Department, of which he was head, and HABS became the joint sponsors of a team to record additional historic buildings in Austin. Assisting Professor Rotsch were Ms. Ellen Beasley, historian, two architects, and four student architects. This group, one of the largest of the summer teams of recent years, concentrated its efforts in the rapidly changing urban area around the Texas State Capitol, recording such structures as the Lundberg Bakery (TEX-3267), the Land Office Building (TEX-397), and several imposing mid- and late nineteenth-century residences, such as the J. H. Houghton House (TEX-3264), which has since been demolished.

A happier disposition was made of the nearby Carrington-Covert House (TEX-3228). Threatened with demolition in 1968, it was saved largely through citizen participation and preservation activity and was subsequently restored. It serves admirably as the headquarters for the Texas State Historical Survey Committee, the agency responsible for National Register programs in the State. Under the leadership of Mr. Truett Latimer, Executive

Land Office, Austin/Arthur Stewart, Photo 1936

Director, this committee has done impressive work toward the recognition and preservation of Texas' heritage from the past.

Forty years have elapsed since the first HABS records were made in Texas. Much of the State's rich architectural heritage has been documented during these years, but much remains to be done. The Historic American Buildings Survey will continue to seek to record the many and diverse structures which are significant examples of Texas architecture. The Survey invites the interest and support of all users of this catalog to assist in this undertaking.

THE HABS TEXAS CATALOG

This catalog contains entries for structures representing the total number of buildings in Texas recorded by the Historic American Buildings Survey through 1974. Entries from the national 1941 *Catalog* and the 1959 *Supplement* have been updated and expanded to provide more useful information; they reflect more clearly the nature and extent of the HABS records, the architectural and historical significance of the structure, and the historical information which has become available. In preparing this catalog, the compiler visited most of the structures listed, verified the addresses, noted the present status or condition, amplified the catalog descriptions of earlier records, and composed new catalog entries for more recently produced records.

Structures are alphabetically arranged according to (a) city or vicinity and (b) the name of the structure. Addresses for most buildings listed in the two earlier catalogs have been expanded, and in a few cases corrected. It is often difficult to give a satisfactory address to structures in a rural or thinly settled area. Buildings in or near smaller towns and communities have been listed together under the name of the town (e.g., ANDERSON AND VICINITY). In larger urban areas with more definite boundaries, a distinction is made between buildings in the city and those in the immediate area (e.g., AUSTIN, AUSTIN VICINITY).

As far as possible, the entries reflect the latest historical research. In many cases it has been possible to correct dates for buildings or note them more precisely and fully. In some cases more historically accurate names have been assigned, with cross references under formerly used names where necessary. Care has been taken to avoid making or repeating errors, but if the reader notices any, HABS will greatly appreciate receiving corrections.

The purpose of this catalog is to present concise descriptions of structures and the HABS records of each, sufficiently informative to prospective users for them to find data they desire and to order duplicates from the Library of Congress.

The format for the entries consists of: the historic name; HABS number; address; brief description, including construction materials, dimensions, number of stories, roof type, and important interior and exterior details; date of erection; architect, if known; alterations and additions; and a listing of the measured drawings, photographs, photocopies, and pages of data available in the HABS archives.

Appended to the catalog is a listing of the Historic American Buildings Survey Inventory forms for Texas. The inventory recording program, which utilized a brief one-page form, operated between 1953 and 1970. It was designed to broaden the coverage of the Survey by allowing interested laymen and professionals to donate a minimum amount of information on a variety of structures. The forms are now on file in the Library of Congress where they form a companion collection for the HABS records.

The following abbreviations and symbols have been used in all of the recent Historic American Buildings Survey catalogs:

TEX-100   Historic American Buildings Survey number. All structures recorded by the Survey are assigned a HABS number. These numbers have no historical significance but serve only to facilitate

	processing. These numbers should be used when inquiring about a structure or ordering a reproduction.
"Sheets"	indicates the number of sheets of measured drawings available for study and reproduction. Sheets are a standard size, 15½" x 20" inside border lines. The number of sheets in the set and the kinds of drawings (plans, elevations, sections, details) are listed. Prints of measured drawings are made at actual size.
"Photos"	("ext. photos" and "int. photos"). HABS negatives normally are 5"x7" (sometimes other sizes, especially 4"x5" or 8"x10"). Duplicate prints of HABS photographs are the same size as the originals.
"Data Pages"	It is HABS policy to give the physical history of the structure along with a technical architectural description. Original data pages are typewritten and may be duplicated.
"HABSI"	HABS Inventory forms. These single-page records have usually been made through the collaboration of the American Institute of Architects. A standard form provides for identification of the structure, concise written historical and/or architectural data, a small photograph, location diagram and source references. HABSI forms are duplicated at actual size (8"x10½").
n.d.	the date is not ascertainable.
*	an asterisk after a date indicates that the measured drawings, photographs, or data pages made on the indicated date are temporarily being held for editing and processing at the Washington, D.C. office of the Historic American Buildings Survey.
NHL	The building has been declared a National Historic Landmark.
NR	The building has been entered on the National Register of Historic Places.

General Thomas Jefferson Chambers House, Anahuac/
Harry L. Starnes, Photo 1936

Chambers, General Thomas Jefferson, House (TEX-281)
Cummings Street at Washington Avenue

Wooden frame, board and batten, 24' (three-bay front) x
32', two stories, gabled roof with broad overhang, galleried
porches front and rear. Large circular window in gable end
has muntins in shape of five-point star. Exterior spiral stair
rising from front porch gives only access to second floor.
The two rooms of equal size on each floor have interior
board and batten walls. Built 1845 for Virginia-born General
Chambers, whose service to Texas began in 1829 under
Mexican rule. In 1861 he was a member of the Texas
Secession Convention. In 1865, an assassin, aiming through
a window, killed Chambers as he sat inside this house.
3 sheets (1936, including plans, elevations, details); 4 ext.
photos (1936), 1 int. photo (1936); 2 data pages (1936).

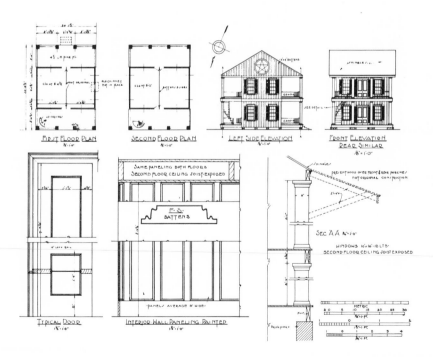

Chambers House/I. L. Day, Del. 1936

Baptist Church (TEX-276)
Main Street

Stone, once stuccoed with imitation stone joints, three-bay front, gabled roof, gable ends of board; square, flat-roofed belfry. Built 1844 by slave labor, burned 1850, rebuilt 1855. Site of organization meeting of the Texas Baptist Convention and of the first Baptist publication in Texas. Also used for Masonic meetings. 2 ext. photos (1936); 1 data page (1936).

Barnes, General James W., Plantation House ("Prairie Woods") (TEX-287)
E. of Anderson 2½ miles, via Farm Road 1774.

Wooden frame, 64'5" (five-bay front) x 33'9", two stories, hipped-roof rectangle, pedimented two-story front entrance porch, lean-to additions at rear. A two-story log house built in 1842 was refinished to become part of the mansion completed in 1858, now in poor state of repair. Builder James W. Barnes, a successful planter, served as Brigadier General in the Confederate Army. 8 sheets (meas. 1963, drawn 1964, including site plan, plans, elevations, details); 4 ext. photos (1933); 5 data pages (1964). HABSI.

General James W. Barnes Plantation House, Anderson Vicinity/
Mike Greer, Del. 1936

Black-Schroder Springhouse (Neblett Springhouse) (TEX-220)
Gone.

Stone, quarried and dry-laid, one story, gabled roof with overhang at gable end. Built, along with a log house, by John S. Black on a land grant of 1831. Springhouse outlasted, for a time, the log house which it served. 1 ext. photo (1936) ; 1 data page (1936).

Boggess, H. H., House (TEX-221)
Fanthorp Street near Farm Road 1774.

Wooden frame with clapboarding, three-bay front, two stories, gabled roof with two-story entrance porch on gable-end facade, unusual in Texas. Built in 1850 by H. H. Boggess, merchant and land speculator. 1 ext. photo (1936) ; 1 data page (1936).

Bowman House (Bowman-Clarke-Kelley House) (TEX-272)
Four miles W. of Anderson, not easily accessible.

Wooden frame with clapboarding, two-bay front, one story, gabled roof extends over six-post front porch, chimney at each gable end. Built 1830 by John Bowman of Kentucky, an early friend of Stephen F. Austin and a political leader of Texas' colonial period. 1 ext. photo (1936) ; 1 data page (1936).

Buchanan, Dr. J. E., House (TEX-223)
Gone.

Wooden frame with clapboarding, three-bay front, two stories, hipped roof, provincial classic entablature over two-story entrance porch. Built by Dr. Buchanan, physician and politician, who came to Anderson from Alabama in the late 1850's. 1 ext. photo (1936) ; 1 data page (1936).

Cawthorn, E. W., House (Womack House) (TEX-274)
Off Farm Road 149.

Wooden frame with clapboarding, five-bay front, two stories, gabled roof, chimney at each gabled end, one-story entrance porch across front, lean-tos and gabled ell at rear. A later gabled room above porch has been removed recently, bringing the house closer to its original appearance. 2 ext. photos (1936).

Dickson, David C., House (TEX-273)
Farm Road 1774.

Wooden frame and clapboarding, three-bay front, two stories, gabled roof, chimney at each gable end, two-story gabled entrance porch. Built 1848 for David C. Dickson, an early Texas congressman and Lieutenant Governor (1853-55). Poor condition. 2 ext. photos (1936) ; 1 data page (1937).

Fanthorp Tavern (TEX-217)
South Main Street

Wooden frame with clapboarding, five-bay front, two stories, gabled roof, L-plan. Built c. 1834 by Henry Fanthorp of England. Two stagecoach lines met in front of the house, which became known as Fanthorp Inn. Parts of this commodious hostelry were razed at an early date leaving a large private residence, now restored. When Kenneth L. Anderson, last Vice-President of the Republic of Texas, died at this Inn in 1845, the citizens of Fanthorp renamed their town "Anderson" in his honor. 2 ext photos (1936) ; 1 data page (1936).

Fuqua, Ephraim, House (TEX-275)
Gone. Originally located S. of Anderson on old La Bahia Road.

Log, two-bay front, one story, double-pitched gabled roof extended over recessed two-post entrance porch, rock chimney at one gable end. Built 1858 by Ephraim Fuqua from Louisiana, a planter and merchant. 1 ext. photo (1936) ; 1 data page (1936).

Green, Allen, House (TEX-218)
Gone.

Cedar logs and wooden frame with clapboarding, five-bay front, two stories, gabled roof, L-plan, native stone chimney. Built 1840. 1 ext. photo (1936) ; 1 data page (1936).

Neblett Springhouse (See *Black-Schroder Springhouse*)

Pahl, Henry, House (TEX-219)
Gone.

Wooden frame, four-bay front, one story, broad gabled roof, recessed porches front and rear, native stone chimney at one gable end. Built 1840. 1 ext. photo (1936); 1 data page (1936).

"Prairie Woods" (See *Barnes, General James W., Plantation House*)

Womack House (See *Cawthorn, E. W., House*)

ANGLETON VICINITY   Brazoria County (20)

Chenango Sugar Mill (TEX-283)
10 miles NW. of Angleton, not easily accessible

Brick, 50'x120', one and two stories, wood-trussed gabled roofs. Part of an extensive plantation established in the 1830's by Edwards (of New York) and Dart (of New Orleans), and operated for a time as a link in a slave-smuggling operation. Built by Monroe Edwards. Condition ruinous. 3 sheets (1936, including site plan, plans, elevations, details); 1 ext. photo (1936); 1 data page (1936).

AUSTIN   Travis County (227)

Bremond, Eugene, House (TEX-3143)
404 W. 7th St.

Wooden frame with clapboarding, one story with raised basement, surrounding porches with square, delicate, paired columns, corresponding paired brackets at cornice. Said to be the oldest house in the "Bremond Block," a residential development of the Bremond and Robinson families dating from the 1860's to the 1890's. 2 ext. photos (1961); 3 data pages (1965). NR (included in Bremond Block Historic District).

Bremond, John, House (TEX-3140)
W. 7th and Guadalupe Streets

Brick and stone, 60′ (four-bay front) x 67′, two-and-a-half stories, mansard roof, two-story entrance porch with ornamental iron railings and crestings. Richly ornamented interiors are organized around large central stair hall. Built 1887 by George Fiegel. 5 ext. photos (1965), 5 int. photos (1965); 5 data pages (1965). NR (included in Bremond Block Historic District).

John Bremond House, Austin/Jack E. Boucher, Photo 1965

John Bremond House, Austin/Jack E. Boucher, Photo 1965

Carrington-Covert House (TEX-3228)
1511 Colorado St., SE. corner Colorado and W. 14th Streets

Limestone, coursed and dressed with quoins, L-shape, five-bay front, two stories, low hipped roof, two-story rear gallery in ell. Center hall plan. Built 1853-57. Restored 1971-73 for use as headquarters and offices of Texas State Historical Survey Committee. One of last remaining residential buildings in area around Texas State Capitol. 10 ext. photos (1974*), 1 int. photo (1974*). NR.

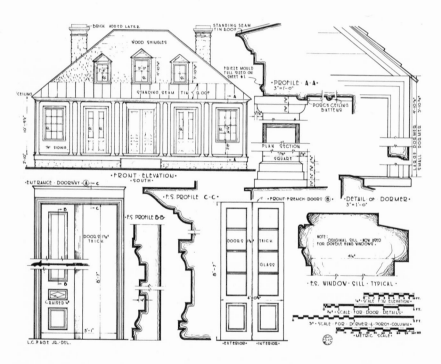

French Legation to Republic of Texas, Austin/L. C. Page, Jr., Del. 1934

French Legation to Republic of Texas (TEX-33-C-1)
7th and San Marcos Streets

Museum. Wooden frame with clapboarding, 42' (five-bay front) x 42', one-and-a-half stories, hipped roof, three gabled dormers and five-bay veranda with square, paired columns. Built 1841 for Count Alphonse de Saligny, representative of

France to the Republic of Texas. It is the only building of the foreign embassies which still exists in Texas. Later altered, but subsequently restored by the Daughters of the Republic of Texas. The separate kitchen has been reconstructed at the rear. 4 sheets (1934, including site plan, plans, elevations, section, details) ; 5 ext. photos (1934), 6 ext. photos (1961*), 3 int. photos (1961*) ; 3 data pages (1936). NR.

General Land Office (See *Land Office*)

Gethsemane Lutheran Church (TEX-3137)
16th Street and Congress Avenue

Buff brick, 37'x74', small apse, steep gabled roof, rectangular plan, Gothic Revival detail. Balcony-organ loft at rear of nave. Built 1883 for earliest Swedish Lutheran congregation in Texas (organized 1868). 6 sheets (1961, including site plan, plans, elevations, sections, details) ; 6 ext. photos (1961), 1 int. photo of window (1961) ; 4 data pages (1961). NR.

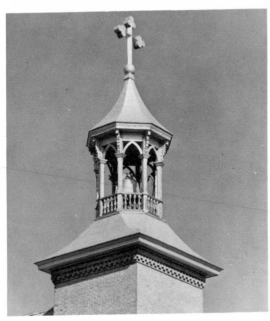

Gethsemane Lutheran Church, Austin/Jack E. Boucher, Photo 1961

47

Goodman Building, Austin/Robert D. Ferland, Del. 1973

Goodman Building (TEX-3263)
202 W. 13th St., NW. corner 13th and Colorado Streets

Brick, 69'5" (ten-bay front) x 53'9", two stories, slightly sloping roof hidden by parapets on three sides, two-tiered porch on S. front. Built c. 1893 as grocery store and saloon on first floor with schoolrooms on second floor. Remodeled 1939 for use as offices and apartments. Good example of late 19th-century commercial architecture in Austin. 7 sheets (1973*, including site plan, plans, elevations, section, details); 1 ext. photocopy (n.d.), 4 ext. photos (1974*); 13 data pages (1973*). NR.

Governor's Mansion, Austin/Jack E. Boucher, Photo 1966

Governor's Mansion (TEX-33-C-4)
Colorado and 11th Streets

Brick, painted white, 58' (five-bay front) x 59', two stories, low hipped roof concealed by entablature, six-column Ionic portico with delicate pine railing at first and second story decks. Greek Revival detail. Center hall plan with curving stair. Built 1853-55. Abner Cook, architect. Rear extension added 1914. 11 sheets (1936, including site plan, plans, elevations, details) ; 16 ext. photos (1934), 9 ext. photos (1966*), 8 int. photos (1966*), 1 ext. photo of garage (1934) ; 1 data page (1934). NR.

Governor's Mansion/Jack E. Boucher, Photo 1966

Houghton, J. H., House (TEX-3264)
Gone. Originally 307 W. 12th St., SE. corner 12th and Guadalupe Streets.

Pressed yellow brick above rock-faced ashlar limestone foundation, L-shaped, 57'3" x 71'4", two-and-a-half stories, complex roof with ridged and hipped projections with dormers, one story front and side porches, square three-and-a-half story tower over entrance, round two-and-a-half story tower at NW. corner, elaborate sheet metal cornice. Irregular plan. Built 1886-87 for John H. Houghton, prominent Austin businessman. James Wahrenberger, architect; Charles A. Shurr, builder. One of the most elaborate of Austin's late 19th-century mansions. Demolished 1973. 8 sheets (1973*, including site plan, plans, elevations, sections, details); 1 ext. photocopy (1890's); 3 ext. photocopies showing this and neighboring Taylor-Hunnicutt House (TEX-3268) (1890's); 4 ext. photos (1974*), 4 int. photos (1974*); 14 data pages (1973*). NR.

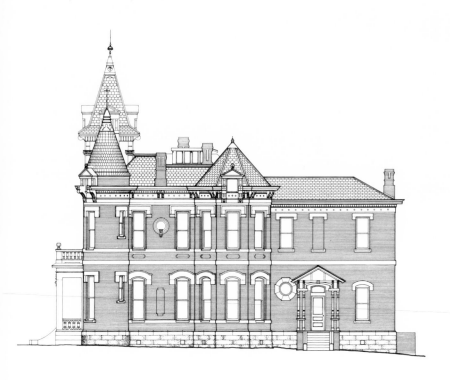

J. H. Houghton House, Austin/J. Tucker Bishop, Del. 1973

EAST ELEVATION

SOUTH ELEVATION

Houghton Carriage House, Austin/Carl J. Frenning, Del. 1973

Houghton Carriage House (TEX-3264-A)
Rear of 307 W. 12th St., fronting on Guadalupe.

Brick, 24' x 44', one-and-a-half stories, mansard roof, cupola with louvers and pyramidal roof. Built c. 1890. Addition (21' x 12') built 1946. A service building of the Houghton House, and related to it in design. It now serves as a blueprint office. 3 sheets (1973*, including site plan, plans, elevations) ; 5 ext. photos (1974*) ; 9 data pages (1973*).

House (TEX-3266)
504 W. 14th St., between Nueces and San Antonio Streets.

Pressed yellow brick with rubble ledge limestone foundation, cut limestone quoins, 38' (five-bay front) x 30'7", one story, hipped roof with deck edged with sheet metal cresting, front porch. Built c. 1883, attributed to James Baird Smith, architect-builder, who may have used stone from the Old Texas State Capitol (burned 1881) in its construction. Later rear additions. Typical small, stone, late 19th-century Austin residence. 6 sheets (1973*, including site plan, plans, elevations, sections, details) ; 4 ext. photos (1974*), 2 int. photos (1974*) ; 14 data pages (1973*).

House, 504 W. 14th Street, Austin/Photo 1974

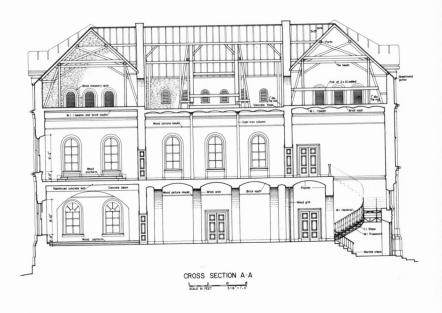

CROSS SECTION A·A

SCALE IN FEET   3/16" = 1'-0"

Land Office, Austin/J. Tucker Bishop. Del. 1973

Land Office (General Land Office) (TEX-397)
108 E. 11th St., near SE. corner of Texas State Capitol grounds

Museum. Rubble ledge limestone, stuccoed, 94′2″ (seven-bay front) x 61′2″, two stories and attic, gable roof in H-plan, Romanseque detail ("Rundbogenstil"); ornamental open stair at south end, enclosed secondary spiral stone stair near center of building. Built 1856-57. Conrad C. Stremme, a professor of architecture in Germany and court counselor to Russian Emperor Nicholas I before immigrating to Texas, architect. Q. Nichols and William Baker, builders. Alterations 1863; 1882 (new stairway); 1884-86; 1892-94; renovated for use as museum 1918-19 (Dennis Walsh, architect); 1958 (August Watkins Harris, architect); 1964. The General Land Office was established by the Republic of Texas in 1837 to survey, distribute, and colonize the public domain, the greatest economic resource of the government

54

Land Office/Jack E. Boucher, Photo 1961

and a resource retained by the State in the annexation treaty with the United States. Considered to be first fireproof building in Texas. Wm. Sydney Porter (O. Henry) was a draftsman in the building from 1887-91. 8 sheets (1973*, including site plan, plans, elevations, sections) ; 4 ext. photos (1936), 9 ext. photos (1961), 4 ext. photos (1974*), 2 int. photos (1936), 7 int. photos (1974*) ; 1 ext. photocopy (1873), 2 ext. photocopies (1890's), 1 photocopy of bird's-eye view (1887), 1 photocopy of architect's drawing of N. elev. (1854), 1 int. photocopy (1887) ; 2 data pages (1937), 3 data pages (1965), 17 data pages (1973*, including copies of 1856 specifications) ; HABSI. NR.

Lundberg Bakery (TEX-3267)
1006 Congress Ave., between W. 10th and W. 11th Streets.

Brick trimmed with limestone (facade), stone and brick side and rear walls, 21'5" (three-bay front) x 158'8" (including several rear additions), two stories, ridge roof behind parapet-type masonry gables at front and rear of original portion. Stone eagle tops front gable. Open plan. Built 1875-76 by Anton Schaefer for Charles Lundberg as ice cream parlor and bakery. Rear addition 1880. 5 sheets (1973*, including site plan, plans, elevations, section, details); 1 ext. photocopy (1890's); 6 int. photocopies (n.d.); 3 ext. photos (1974*), 2 int. photos (1974*); 14 data pages (1973*). NR.

Lundberg Bakery, Austin/David J. Yturralde, Del. 1973

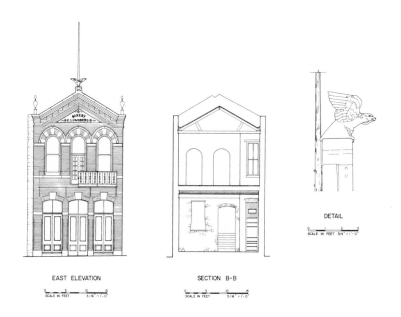

EAST ELEVATION

SCALE IN FEET 3/16" = 1'-0"

SECTION B-B

SCALE IN FEET 3/16" = 1'-0"

DETAIL

SCALE IN FEET 3/4" = 1'-0"

Lundberg Bakery/David J. Yturralde, Del. 1973

Millett Mansion (TEX-3142)
Gone. Formerly at 9th and Brazos Streets.

Brick with stone quoins, three stories, hipped roofs, one-story porch at front of middle level, slope of site permitted three-story gallery along side. C. F. Millett, whose lumber-yard was adjacent, built the mansion about 1880 to be used as a boardinghouse. Razed 1963. 2 ext. photos (1961); 3 data pages (1965).

Neill-Cochran House (TEX-3239)
2310 San Gabriel St., between W. 23rd and W. 24th Streets.

Museum. Local limestone rubble, 51'4" (five-bay front) x 47'5", two stories, roof concealed by broad entablature, monumental hexastyle Doric portico, delicate-railed balcony over entrance, center hall plan, Greek Revival. Built about

1853; Abner Cook, architect. Though built for Green Washington Hill, the house takes the name of two prominent families who later owned it. Now owned and maintained by the National Society of the Colonial Dames of America in the State of Texas. 13 sheets (n.d.*, including site plan, plans, elevations, details). NR.

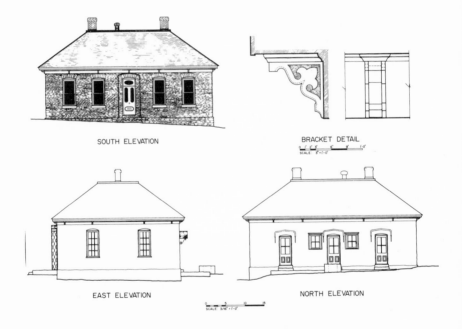

SOUTH ELEVATION

BRACKET DETAIL

EAST ELEVATION

NORTH ELEVATION

Orsay Tenant House, Austin/Richard W. Schreiber, Del. 1973

Orsay Tenant House (TEX-3265)
310 E. 14th St., NW. corner E. 14th and Trinity Streets.

Rubble ledge limestone, 42'9" (five-bay front) x 31'5", one story, hipped roof with deck. Built mid-1870's. Small vernacular residence, one of few remaining of its type in the Capitol district. 4 sheets (1973*, including site plan, plan, elevations, section, details); 3 ext. photos (1974*); 11 data pages (1973*). NR.

Pease, Governor Elisha M., Mansion ("Woodlawn") (TEX-330)
6 Niles Road

Brick, five-bay front, two stories, low hipped roof concealed by broad entablature, six-column Ionic portico, delicate balcony above front entrance, Greek Revival detail. Built before 1853 by Abner Cook for James C. Shaw. Shaw occupied it only briefly before he sold the house to Governor Elisha M. Pease, whose descendants lived in the house until its purchase by Governor Allan Shivers in 1956. 7 ext. photos (1936), 1 int. photo (1936) ; 2 data pages (1937). NR.

Raymond, Nathaniel, House (TEX-331)
Gone. Formerly 204 E. 24th St.

Brick and stucco, 53'4" (five-bay front) x 59'5", two stories, original portion hipped roof with balustrade on deck; two-story entrance porch. Center hall plan, graceful stair. Built 1857, remodeled and extended 1893. Razed in 1950's. 7 sheets (1936, including site plan, plans, elevations, sections, details) ; 6 ext. photos (1936) ; 2 data pages (1937).

Simms-Vance House (TEX-33-C-3)
Gone. Formerly at 1802 San Gabriel St.

Limestone ashlar stuccoed and ruled in regular stone pattern, 55' x 52', two stories, sloping site presents E. front elevation as one story, hipped roof, entrance porch with six square columns across front. Center hall plan, parlor on entrance level with bedrooms, dining room on lower floor. First portion built 1859, 20' x 36' ell added 1880. The house was built for Milton W. Simms by 1860; Vance acquired it 1908. 9 sheets (1936, including plans, elevations, sections, details) ; 4 ext. photos (1934) ; 1 data page (1936).

Taylor-Hunnicutt House (TEX-3268)
405 W. 12th St., between San Antonio and Guadalupe Streets.

Hand-dressed ashlar limestone with quoins, 51'3" (five-bay front) x 79'4" (including rear ell), two-and-a-half stories, mansard roof with dormers, two-tiered front porch with paired posts, bracketed cornice; center hall plan. Built 1872 fronting on Guadalupe St.; moved to adjoining lot fronting

W. 12th St., 1925. Second level of porch later addition. Dormers also modified. 4 sheets (1973*, including site plan, plans, elevations, details) ; 3 ext. photocopies listed under neighboring Houghton House (TEX-3264) ; 1 bird's-eye perspective of area (1873) ; 4 ext. photos (1974*), 3 int. photos (1974*) ; 10 data pages (1973*).

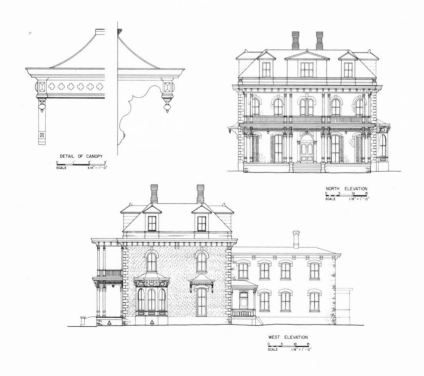

Taylor-Hunnicutt House, Austin/David J. Yturralde, Del. 1973

Texas State Capitol (TEX-3326)
State Capitol Grounds, head of Congress Avenue

Texas pink granite, 566'6" x 289', four stories and raised basement, three-story arch shelters main entrance. Circular dome 250' from basement floor to base of lantern. Legislative chambers occupy symmetrical wings on each side of a rotunda richly ornamented with tiered Renaissance detail. Built 1882-88. Elijah E. Myers, architect. Myers, who also designed the capitols of Michigan (1872-79) and Colorado (1890-94), was selected in a competition in 1881 which was judged by Napoleon LeBrun. The construction contract of January 1882 was with Mattheas Schnell of Rock Island, Illinois, for the sum of three million acres on Panhandle land; in June 1882, the contract was transferred to Abner Taylor of Chicago. Capitol building dedicated May 1888. 6 ext. photos (1966*), 13 int. photos (1966*), 1 photocopy of bird's-eye view (1887). NR.

Townsend, Angela, House (TEX-3141)
Gone. Formerly 1802 West Ave.

Coursed native limestone ashlar, 37' (seven-bay front) x 48', two-and-a-half stories, rear ell addition, steep hipped roof with widow's walk and hipped dormers, modillion cornice. Except for a one-story six-column porch across the front, the lines of the house are those of Georgian houses such as might be found in Massachusetts. The childhood home of Angela Townsend. House built about 1870. Razed 1962. 5 ext. photos (1961), 3 data pages (1965).

"Woodlawn" (See *Pease, Governor Elisha M., Mansion*)

AUSTIN VICINITY   Travis County (227)

Sneed, Judge Sebron G., House (TEX-399)
6 miles S. of Austin via I-35 and Bluff Springs Road

Limestone ashlar, 58'4" (seven-bay front) x 40', two stories, gabled roof, double chimney at each gable end. Symmetrical plan with six square rooms on each floor. Judge Sneed, from Arkansas, acquired the 470-acre property in 1854, began construction of the house in 1857 with a mason named Simms and a carpenter named Miles Byrne, and slave labor to quarry the stone. War stopped the work, and the house, never entirely completed, still lacks its intended porches and interior finishes. 8 sheets (1961, including plans, elevations, sections, details); 3 ext. photos (1936), 1 int. photo of mantel (1936); 2 data pages (1937).

BASTROP AND VICINITY   Bastrop County (11)

Crocheron, Henry, House (TEX-335)
1502 Wilson St.

Wooden frame with clapboarding, 35'2" (three-bay front) x 30'3", two stories, flat-roofed front portion, one-story gabled ell at rear. Two-story entrance porch, typical of Bastrop, leads to unusual entrance-reception hall, extending the full width of the house. Built 1857, almost entirely of cedar. 8 sheets (1936, including site plan, plans, elevations, details); 3 ext. photos (1936), 2 int. photos of stair and mantel (1936); 1 data page (1937).

Hill, A. Wiley, House (TEX-336)
5 miles S. of Bastrop on Tex. 304, then E. to Hill's Prairie

Wooden frame with clapboarding, 53' x 44', including full height six-column portico which shelters a balcony over the entrance door, two chimneys at each gable end. 29' x 35' kitchen ell at rear, fluted pilasters at each corner. Center hall plan, open stair with walnut balustrade. A squared volute design ornaments the mantel in the main parlor. Built 1857. 7 sheets (1936, including site plan, plans, elevations, details); 7 ext. photos (1936), 4 int. photos (1936); 1 data page (1936).

Jung-Pearcy House (TEX-3127)
909 Pecan St.

Brick, three-bay front, one story, gabled roof; hipped-roof entrance porch. Rectangular plan. Built c. 1873 by Joseph Jung, whose brickyard produced the moulded brick for the cornice. 2 ext. photos (1937); 1 data page (1937).

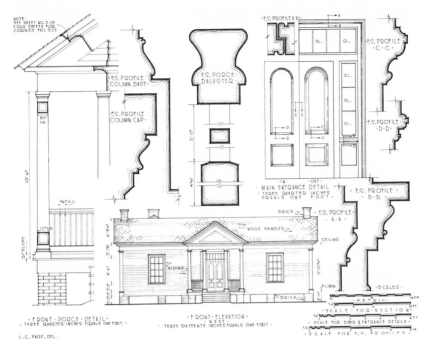

·f.S. PROFILE·X-X·

·f.S. PROFILE·
·C·C·

·f.S. PROFILE
COLUMN BASE·

·f.S. PORCH
BALUSTER·

GL.   GL.

·f.S. PROFILE
COLUMN CAP·

GL.

GL.

·f.S.PROFILE·
·D·D·

·IN· ·OUT·
·MAIN ENTRANCE DETAIL·
·THREE QUARTER INCHES
EQUALS ONE FOOT·

·f.S. PROFILE·
·D-D·

BRICK · f.S. PROFILE·
·A-A·

WOOD SHINGLES

CEILING

SIDING

BRICK

FLOOR

·SCALES·

·METRIC·

·SCALE·FOR·SECTION·

·FRONT·PORCH·DETAIL·
·THREE QUARTER INCHES EQUALS ONE FOOT·

·FRONT·ELEVATION·
·WEST·
·THREE SIXTEENTH INCHES EQUALS ONE FOOT·

·SCALE FOR DOOR & ENTRANCE DETAILS·

·SCALE FOR F.S. PROFILES·

L.C. PAGE, DEL.

Governor Joseph D. Sayers House, Bastrop/L. C. Page, Del. 1934

Sayers, Governor Joseph D., House (TEX-33-C-5)
1703 Wilson St.

Wooden frame with clapboarding, 50'4" (three-bay front) x 50'6", one story, low gabled roof, pedimented entrance porch. Center hall plan with rear ell. A simple, beautifully proportioned bachelor's cottage. Joseph D. Sayers was 27 years old and had returned from four years' service in the Confederate Army when he had this house built in 1868. He served as State Senator, Lieutenant Governor and for 14 years in the U.S. Congress before he became Governor of Texas in 1899, a post he filled for two terms. 4 sheets (1934, including site plan, plans, elevations, section, and details); 6 ext. photos (1934); 2 data pages (1936).

Wilbarger House (TEX-33-C-6)
1403 N. Main St.

Wooden frame with clapboarding, 46'3" (five-bay front) x 58'11", two stories, with one-story extensions at rear, low gabled roof, two-story entrance porch. Center hall plan. Built 1852, later additions and alterations. 5 sheets (1934, including plans, elevations, sections, details) ; 6 ext. photos (1934) ; 1 data page (1934).

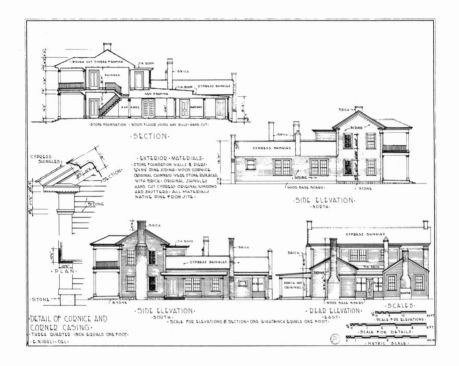

Wilbarger House, Bastrop/E. Niggli, Del. 1934

BELMONT VICINITY

Gonzales County (89)

King, Tom, House (TEX-352)
Gone.

Adobe, two stories, gabled roof, with large one-story entrance porch across front. Built by Jerry Roberts in 1853 for Tom King, a breeder and trainer of race horses. 4 ext. photos (1936) ; 1 data page (1937).

BOERNE VICINITY

Schertz House (Becker House) (TEX-375)
3.5 miles NE. of Boerne via Farm Road 474 and Spring
Creek Road

Log and stone, five-bay front, one story, gabled roof; shed-
roofed stone addition and lean-to four-post porch along front.
Built 1855, much remodeled since 1936. A log smokehouse
stands nearby. 4 ext. photos (1936), 1 ext photo of smokehouse (1936); 1 data page (1937).

BOVINA VICINITY

Las Escarbadas Ranch House (TEX-3229)
In the SW. corner of Deaf Smith County, about 1 mile E. of
the Texas-New Mexico state line, on Tierra Blanca Draw;
approx. 16 miles NW. of Bovina.

Limestone, undressed, stuccoed, painted to simulate stone
joints, 68'8" x 17'5", two stories, gabled roof with chimneys
at each end and one-story hip-roofed porch. Built into slope.
Interior rooms in linear plan. Built late 1880's. 5 sheets
(1971, including site plan, plans, elevations, section, details).

BRAZORIA

McCormick House (McCormick-Ashcomb House) (TEX-
249)
Gone.

Wooden frame, two stories with one-story ell at rear, gabled
roofs, two-story gallery across front. Built 1859 for Judge
Andrew P. McCormick. 2 ext. photos (1936); 1 data page
(1936).

BROWNSVILLE AND VICINITY

Carmen Ranch House (TEX-33-AB-3)
Gone.

Brick, one story, single slope roof concealed by broad parapet
cornice, rectangular plan with symmetrical openings. El

Carmen Ranch, about nine miles up the Rio Grande from Brownsville, was the headquarters of Juan Cortina, whose bandits captured the city in 1859. 4 sheets (1934, including plan, elevations, details); 7 ext. photos (1934); 1 data page (1934).

Church of the Immaculate Conception (TEX-3139)
12th and Jefferson Streets

Brick, painted, 50' x 150', gabled roof, square entrance tower, buttresses, lancet windows. Gothic Revival detail. Completed in 1859 from a design by Father Pierre Yveres Keralum (Peter Kalum) of Quimper, Brittany, who had studied architecture in Paris before becoming a missionary of the Oblates of Mary Immaculate. Interior restoration necessary in 1970 after severe fire. 6 ext. photos (1961); 7 data pages (1962).

BULLARD AND VICINITY   Smith County (212)

Dewberry, Col. John, Plantation House (TEX-133)
On Farm Road 346, .8 mile N. of Teaselville intersection with Farm Road 344.

Wooden frame with siding, five-bay front, two stories, gabled roof, with pedimented, two-story tetrastyle portico. Classic Revival detail. Center hall plan. Built 1854, as headquarters of a 30,000 acre plantation. 3 ext. photos (1936); 1 data page (1936). HABSI.

Douglas House (TEX-134)
Gone.

Wooden frame with clapboarding, five-bay front, two stories, hipped roof, pedimented two-story entrance porch with railings, square, paired columns at both levels, modillion cornice. Built 1854. 3 ext. photos (1936), 2 int. photos (1936); 1 data page (1936).

Loftin, Alf, House (TEX-135)
Gone. Moved from original site.

Wooden frame with clapboarding, five-bay front, one story,

hipped room, gable-roofed rear addition and shed-roofed recessed rear porch connected to rear porch of house. Built 1848. 3 ext. photos (1936) ; 1 data page (1936).

Loftin, Pitt, House (TEX-132)
5.8 miles W. of Bullard on Farm Road 344.

Wooden frame with clapboarding, five-bay front, one story, hipped roof, deep gabled entrance porch, four small gabled rear and side additions and one gabled side porch. Irregular plan. Built 1859, similar to Alf Loftin House (TEX-135). 3 ext. photos (1937), 1 int. photo (1936) ; 1 data page (1936).

CARTHAGE AND VICINITY   Panola County (183)

Collins, Jasper, House (TEX-15)
Gone.

Wooden frame with clapboarding, five-bay front, one-story over half-basement, hipped roof. Symmetrical plan, Greek Revival detail. Tetrastyle, pedimented portico on front ; nearly identical pedimented porticos at rear and west side. Enclosed shed-roofed porch on east side is recorded as originally a fourth pedimented portico. Built 1850. 4 ext. photos (1936) ; 1 data page (1936).

Morris, Dempsey, House (TEX-17)
Gone.

Wooden frame with clapboarding, one story, gabled roof extending over recessed, four-post front entrance porch ; later attached by small, irregularly-roofed dogrun to a second wooden frame and clapboard, gable-roofed house of greater depth and steeper roof pitch. Begun 1842. 2 ext. photos (1936) ; 1 data page (1936).

Parker, J. B., House (TEX-18)
201 West Sabine

Wooden frame with clapboarding, four-bay front, two stories, gabled roof, railed, two-story, jig-saw-decorated gallery across front, rear ell added. 2 ext. photos (1936) ; 1 data page (1936).

J. B. Parker House, Carthage/Harry Starnes, Photo 1936

Snow House (TEX-16)
Gone.

Wooden frame with clapboarding, one story, gabled roof with off-center ridge and differing front and rear pitches. Built 1840. 2 ext. photos (1936) ; 1 data page (1936).

CASTROVILLE AND VICINITY   Medina County (163)

NOTE: All of the buildings in Castroville are included in the National Register by virtue of being within the boundaries of the Castroville Historic District. The Charles de Montel House, however, is outside the district. The Vance Hotel Complex, in addition to being within the district, is also listed in the National Register as a separate entry.

Bendele, Joe, House (TEX-357)
Angelo Street near Florence Street

Log, one story, gabled roof, rectangular with lean-tos at one end and one side. Thought to have been built prior to 1855, when it was moved from its original site to its present location. 2 ext. photos (1936) ; 1 data page (1936).

Carlé, Andrew, House (TEX-33-A-5)
Main Street at Lafayette Street

Stone and stucco, 37′7″ (four-bay front) x 26′2″, one story, gabled roof with lesser slope extended over two rear rooms. Built 1844 by Henry Castro, the founder of Castroville, and Leopold Menetrier. Sold to Andrew Carlé, 1864. 3 sheets (1934, including site plan, plan, elevations, section, details) ; 1 ext. photo (1934) ; 1 data page (1936).

Carlé, Joseph, House and Store (TEX-390)
Madrid and Angelo Streets (Houston Square)

Stone and stucco, 62′3″ x 85′3″, two stories, gabled roof, with one-story, shed-roofed warehouse at one gable end, and gabled kitchen and dining wing at rear. L-plan. A balcony runs across the second-floor front, supported by metal brackets, and is accessible only through second-floor living quarters. Built in 1850's by Joseph Carlé of Alsace. 5 sheets (1936, including site plan, plans, elevations, sections, details) ; 3 ext. photos (1936), 1 int. photo (1936) ; 1 data page (1936).

Castro, Henry, Storehouse (TEX-356)
Gone.

This storage structure, about the shape and size of a boxcar, was an early example of prefabrication, a frame covered with sheets of zinc about 1/16″ thick, bearing the trademark of a British firm. Count Henri de Castro, signing himself Henri Castro, founded Castroville in 1844. 2 ext. photos (1936) ; 2 data pages (1936).

de Montel, Charles, House (TEX-369)
3 miles NW. of Castroville

Stone and stucco, five-bay front, one story with attic under gabled roof with fanlight at each gable end, pedimented entrance porch. Center hall plan. Originally intended as a two-story house, but when fire destroyed much lumber the plans for second story were omitted. Built 1846 by Charles de Montel (originally Shibenmontel), a German-trained civil engineer, guide for the Castro colony and ultimately Captain in the Confederacy. 7 ext. photos (1936), 2 ext. photos of outbuilding identified as slave quarters (1936); 2 data pages (1936).

First Catholic Church (TEX-359)
Angelo Street between Paris and London Streets

Stone and stucco, 14' x 18', gabled roof. Built 1847. Outgrown upon its completion, it was replaced by a larger church in 1850. 2 ext. photos (1936); 1 data page (1936).

First Lutheran Church (TEX-363)
Gone.

Stone, stucco, and mesquite, gabled roof, rectangular nave built c. 1845, with original tower flush with facade of church; cypress-framed entrance tower and entrance built in 1906. One of the first buildings in Castroville. Builders: August and Andrew Halbardier (stonework), Frank Stindler and Peter Ichorn (carpenters). 2 ext. photos (1936); 1 data page (1936).

Goldberg, C. F., House (TEX-358)
Site unidentifiable.

Wooden frame of heavy oak and cypress, with infilling of field stone, three-bay front, one story, gabled roof with lean-to, two rooms. Built c. 1850 by Xavier Jung for Goldberg, who was from Saxony. 3 ext. photos (1936); 1 data page (1936).

Haass, Louis, House (TEX-367)
Florence Street between Angelo and Amelia Streets

Stone and stucco, three-bay front, one story with attic, gabled roof with shed-roofed lean-tos at both sides joined by hipped-roof rear. Wide French double doors, glazed and paneled. Louvered doors and windows. Built before 1850 by

Gustaf Louis Haass, one of Henri Castro's original colonists. 3 ext. photos (1936); 2 data pages (1936).

Hoog, Peter, House (See *Tondre, Nicolas, House*)

Ihnken, Gerhard, House and Store (TEX-365)
Gone.

Stone and stucco, four-bay front, two stories, gabled roof extended at rear over second-story porch, which rested on a raised rubble-stone barn-basement. Built in 1851 by Gerhard Ihnken of Germany and Holland and his French wife, who was reared on the Marne. Ihnken, who had a contract with the Mexican government for hides and tallow, built his house and store on a cattle trail from Mexico. 4 ext. photos (1936); 1 data page (1936).

Landmark Inn (See *Vance Hotel*)

John Merian House, Castroville/Richard MacAllister, Photo 1936

Merian, John, House (TEX-368)
London and Angelo Streets

Stone and stucco, four-bay front, one-and-a-half stories, high gabled roof. Built 1850's. 3 ext. photos (1936); 1 data page (1936).

Old Courthouse (TEX-364)
Gone. Formerly on the site of the present City Hall.

Stone and stucco, two-bay front, one and two stories, original gabled roof had added false front; roofless and in ruins in 1936 photos. Built 1853, abandoned in 1894 after county seat moved to Hondo in 1892. 2 ext. photos (1936); 1 data page (1936).

Pingenot, P. F., House (TEX-360)
Petersburg Street between Angelo and Lorenzo Streets

Adobe, stuccoed, one story, steep gable levels out over rear portion. Built in early 1850's and sometimes used as a saloon as well as a residence. Originally thatched roof, followed by hand-split shakes. 4 ext. photos (1936), 2 int. photos (1936); 1 data page (1936).

Quintle and Haass Mill (TEX-360)
Millrace, west bank of Medina River S. of Florella Street

Stone and board and batten, one and two stories, gabled roof. Only stone portions of mill remain. When first built in 1854, the corn and flour mill was powered by an undershot water wheel in an open ditch with water from a small dam in the Medina River. Later a water turbine was installed and the ditch covered. 6 ext. photos (1936).

Quintle, Laurent, House and Store (TEX-362)
Gone. Originally near Medina River off Hwy. 90

Stone, 40'5" x 28'4", two stories plus attic and cellar, gabled roof with bracketed eaves, two-story porch 8' wide across rear. Two pairs of double front doors with blind paneling were on the first floor occupied by the store, with the cellar being used for storage; the second story, reached only by outside, rear stairs and porch, was the residence, with small

Laurent Quintle House and Store, Castroville/Zeb Rike, Del. 1936

interior stairs leading to attic. Built c. 1850 by L. Quintle. 6
sheets (1936, including site plan, plans, elevations, sections,
details) ; 3 ext. photos (1936) ; 1 data page (1936).

Simon Cabin (See *Vance Hotel Bathhouse*)

Tarde Hotel (TEX-389)
Florella Street at Madrid Street

Stone and stucco, five-bay front, two stories, gabled roof,
two-story portico with balcony with ornamental wood balustrade over entrance. Built c. 1845 by M. Tarde. 4 ext. photos
(1936), 2 int. photos (1936).

Tondre, Nicolas, House (Peter Hoog House) (TEX-366)
Florence Street at Amelia Street

Stone and stucco, five-bay front, one story with attic, gabled roofs including narrower and lower gabled extension at one end. Built in the early 1840's. Nicolas Tondre's deed to a town lot in Castroville predated the arrival of the colonists. 3 ext. photos (1936) ; 1 data page (1936).

Vance Hotel Bathhouse, Castroville/Max C. Frederick, Photo 1934

Vance Hotel Complex (Landmark Inn) (TEX-33-A-4)
Florence Street at Florella Street

Stone and stucco, 65′ (five-bay front) x 19′7″, two-story hotel, with 20′ x 60′ one-story storeroom ell at rear; gabled roof, two-story rear gallery. Separate 15′ x 18′ kitchen. Portions built before 1853, as home and store, by Caesar Monad; second story added in 1874 by John Vance. A two-story stone bathhouse (Simon Cabin, TEX-354) is also part of the hotel complex. 4 sheets (1934, for Hotel, Storeroom, and Kitchen, including site plan, plans, elevations, sections, details) ; 4 ext. photos of Hotel (1934) ; 3 ext. photos (1934, 1 each of Kitchen, Old Store, and Bathhouse) ; 1 data page for all the structures (1934). NR.

Vance, John, House (TEX-361)
Florella Street behind Vance Hotel

Stone and stucco, two stories, gabled roof, shuttered openings, the sloping site permits an upper level door at one end. Built by John Vance between 1855 and 1860. 4 ext. photos (1936) ; 1 data page (1936).

CENTER VICINITY   Shelby County (210)

Church of the Divine Infant (TEX-266)
Cotton Ford Road

Wooden frame with clapboarding, gabled rectangular form with spire-capped entrance tower. Built in 1847 as Sacred Heart Church in Nacogdoches, it is among the oldest churches in east Texas. Following the construction of a larger church in Nacogdoches, the old building has been moved twice and after a brief career as St. Ann's at Fern Lake, it now serves a small parish in Center. 1 ext. photo (1936) ; 1 data page (1936).

Jones, Louis, House (TEX-12)
Gone.

Log and weatherboard, one story, dog-trot cabin with lean-to porch. Built 1830-36 by Logan Smith. 2 ext. photos (1936) ; 1 data page (1936).

Smith, Emzy C., House (TEX-11)
3 miles NW. of Center and ¼ mile N. of Farm Road 2026

Log covered with board and batten, one story, steep gabled roof with lesser pitch over rear rooms and porch across front. Built 1868. 2 ext. photos (1936) ; 1 data page (1936).

CENTER POINT VICINITY   Kerr County (133)

Ganahl, Dr. Charles, House ("Zanzenburg") (TEX-377)
Gone. Formerly about 1½ miles NE. of Center Point, historic marker at site on Tex. 27

Half-timber with sandstone infilling, 57' (seven-bay front) x 36'4", one story, gabled roof, porch across front; rectangular, six rooms. Built 1857, one of the largest of the early ranch houses, and named Zanzenburg for Ganahl's boyhood home in the Austrian Tyrol. Small, limestone ashlar outbuilding called "fortress" or "Indian House" nearby. Dr. Ganahl, a slaveholder, served the Confederacy as an army surgeon. 5 sheets (1936, including site plan, elevations, and details of house and of "Indian House") ; 6 ext. photos (1936), 2 ext. photos of "Indian House" (1936) ; 1 data page (1936).

CHAPPELL HILL AND VICINITY   Washington County (239)

Browning, Col. William W., House (TEX-265)
0.5 mile S. of intersection of Farm Roads 1155 and 1371

Wooden frame with clapboarding, five-bay front, two stories, hipped roof, square plan with two-story porches at front and rear; center hall plan. Built 1856. 2 ext. photos (1936) ; 1 data page (1936). NR.

Sledge, Col. William Madison, House (John Smith House) (TEX-25)
About 1 mile W. of Chappell Hill

Brick and wood, 49'2" (five-bay front) x 65'9", two-story Palladian design with "piano nobile," hipped roofs, tetrastyle south portico with broad steps rising to entrance level, hexastyle two-story north portico; ground floor wall construction of brick, main floor construction of wood. Built 1850's. Vastly altered by removal of second story. 5 sheets (1936, including site plan, plans, elevations, details); 2 ext. photos (1936); 1 data page (1936).

Smith, John, House (See *Sledge, Col. William Madison, House*)

Stage Coach Tavern (TEX-24)
Farm Road 1155 at Farm Road 2447

Wooden frame with clapboarding, 48' (five-bay front) x 36'4", two stories, hipped roof, Greek fret design on frieze; one story entrance porch. Separate kitchen moved and attached at rear. Built by Jacob Haller and William Hargrove, has copper downspout marked 1851. Operated as inn until the Civil War. 5 sheets (1936, including site plan, plans, elevations, sections, details); 2 ext. photos (1936), 1 int. photo (1936); 1 data page (1936).

FRONT ELEVATION
SOUTH
SCALE ⅛"=1'

Colonel William Madison Sledge House (John Smith House), Chappell Hill/Woodlief F. Brown, Del. 1936

CHERRY SPRING

Rode-Kothe House (TEX-378)
1.3 miles E. of U.S. 87 at Cherry Spring

Limestone, irregular ashlar, five-bay front, three stories, hipped roof, two-story porch on the south, one-story porch on the north. Sited to dominate its surroundings. Built by Dietrich Rode in 1855. 6 ext. photos (1934), 1 int. photo (1936); 1 data page (1937).

Rode-Kothe Sheep Barn (TEX-33-A-14)
1.3 miles E. of U.S. 87 at Cherry Spring

Limestone, irregular ashlar, with board and batten, single-bay gable-end facade, shallow gabled roof, outer stairs to second-floor entrance door at gable end; shed-roofed board and batten lean-to at rear, with entrance door on side, near bottom of stairs. Said to be the first structure built by Dietrich Rode in a complex of buildings including another barn, a blacksmith shop, smokehouse, a large stone water tank or cistern, and residence. 5 ext. photos (1934), 2 int. photos (1934); 1 data page (1934).

CHIRENO VICINITY

Old Half-Way Inn (TEX-33-D-5)
2 miles W. of Chireno on Tex. 21

Wooden frame with clapboarding, 50' (five-bay front) x 29', two stories, shallow gabled roof, chimney at each gable end; two-story front porch has columns of heavy boards held rigid by spacer blocks, creating an openwork design. Built prior to 1837 by James B. Johnson, who was operating it by that date as a half-way station on the stagecoach route between San Augustine and Nacogdoches. 4 sheets (1934, including plans, elevations, details); 5 ext. photos (1934), 1 ext. photo (1936); 1 data page (1936).

CLARENDON VICINITY

Bairfield School (See LUBBOCK, Lubbock County)

CLAUDE VICINITY

"J A" Milk and Meat Cooler (See LUBBOCK, Lubbock County)

COLUMBUS AND VICINITY

Tait Plantation House (TEX-282)
10 miles S. of Columbus via Tex. 71, county, and private roads

Log, covered with board and batten, three-bay front, two stories, gabled roof with stone chimneys each end, shed-roofed porch across front, newer addition at rear. Built 1847 by Dr. Charles W. Tait, engineer and physician, whose ranch on the Colorado River numbered 1900 acres by that time. The house has been moved and remodeled but retains some of its early character. It remains the ranch headquarters of the Tait family. A slave cabin and early barn have been reconstructed nearby. 2 sheets (1936, including site plan, plans, elevations, sections); 3 ext. photos (1936); 1 data page (1936).

Tait Town House (TEX-250)
526 Wallace St.

Wooden frame, five-bay front, two stories, plus attic and basement, gabled roof with central widow's walk platform, two brick chimneys at each end, pedimented distyle porch shelters second-story balcony above entrance. Begun in 1856 by Dr. Charles W. Tait, who selected the location to remove his family from the less healthful lowlands of his plantation house. 3 ext. photos (1936); 1 data page (1936).

COMFORT

Faltin House (TEX-376)
7th Street NE. of Main Street

Half-timber with cut limestone and adobe brick infilling, once stuccoed, 31' (five-bay front) x 24', steep gabled roof, front porch. Like the roofs of other houses in the German-settled area of Texas, this one breaks to a steeper pitch as it approaches the roof line. Built 1854 by M. T. Goldbeck. 4 sheets (1936, including site plan, plan, elevations, details); 3 ext. photos, which also show elaborate jigsawn well canopy (1936); 1 data page (1936).

CORPUS CHRISTI   Nueces County (178)

Meuly, Conrad, House and Store (TEX-3114)
Gone. Formerly 210 Chaparral St.

Oyster shell concrete, 31'3" (four-bay front) x 40'11" hipped roof, two stories, elaborate ornamental iron gallery across front, wooden gallery with exterior stairs at rear. Store occupied only front portion of lower floor. Built 1852-54 by Conrad Meuly, a Swiss merchant who had come to Texas in 1833. 7 sheets (1936, including site plan, plans, elevations, details, especially of ironwork); 10 ext. photos (c. 1919), 6 ext. photos (1936); 2 data pages (1937).

FRONT (WEST) ELEVATION
SCALE ³⁄₁₆" = 1'-0"

Conrad Meuly House and Store, Corpus Christi/ Charles H. Bertrand and Zeb Rike, Del. 1936

Collins, Tom, House (See *"Park Hill"*)

Monroe-Coleman House (TEX-232)
707 E. Houston St.

Wooden frame with clapboarding, five-bay front, one-and-a-half stories with raised basement, gabled rectangle with twin chimneys at each end, pedimented entrance porch. Center hall plan. Built in 1854 for A. T. Monroe, nephew of President James Monroe. Architect may have been John McVey. Sold to Daniel Coleman before 1860. 2 ext. photos (1936) ; 1 data page (1936). NR.

"Park Hill" (Tom Collins House) (TEX-233)
1 mile W. of Crockett, between Farm Roads 229 and 2076

Wooden frame with clapboarding, one-and-a-half stories, gabled roof, hexastyle entrance porticos at both gabled ends, with large, railed openings in the pediments above. Built 1854. 2 ext. photos (1936), 1 int. photo (1936) ; 1 data page (1936), 1 data page (1937).

CUEVITAS   Jim Hogg County (124)

Roderíguez, Eugenio, House and Post Office (TEX-3138)
Farm Road 649

Limestone, stuccoed, 34' (two-bay front) x 34', one story, gabled roof, gabled ends with low parapet, porch along east side. Frame Post Office addition built soon after main buildings, probably between 1850 and 1875; abandoned in the early 1930's. The simplicity of the structure reflects the remoteness and austerity of early ranch life. 5 ext. photos (1962) ; 4 data pages (1962).

Eugenio Roderíguez House, Cuevitas/W. Eugene George, Photo 1961

CZESTOCHOWA   Karnes County (128)

Nativity of the Blessed Virgin Mary Church (TEX-3240)
¼ mile W. of Tex. 123

Local limestone, originally 48' x 76', pinnacled buttresses
mark five-bay aisleless nave, copper-spired entrance tower.
Gothic Revival. Dedicated February 1878. Tower height
increased one story to 99'5" and apse and transepts added in
1930, bringing overall length to 138'5" and width to 72'. The
Parish of Czestochowa was formed in 1874 by 40 families
who separated themselves from the original Polish Catholic
settlements in America at Panna Maria, five miles to the
southeast. 6 sheets (1971*, including site plan, plan, elevations, section) ; 8 data pages (1971*).

Pawelek, Machie, House (See PAWELEKVILLE)

Nativity of the Blessed Virgin Mary Church, Czestochowa/
Thomas E. Ferrell, Del. 1971

DALLAS

Dallas County (57)

Morehead-Gano Log House (TEX-3269)
Old City Park. Originally on Tex. 121, NW. of intersection
with Bethel Road.

House museum. Log, covered with weatherboarding, 41' x
34', one-and-a-half stories, gable roof. Originally a dog-trot
plan. Built early 1850's, porch, loft and shed addition c.
1858. Relocated and restored 1974 by Dallas County Heritage Society. 5 sheets (1974, including site plan, plans, elevations, sections).

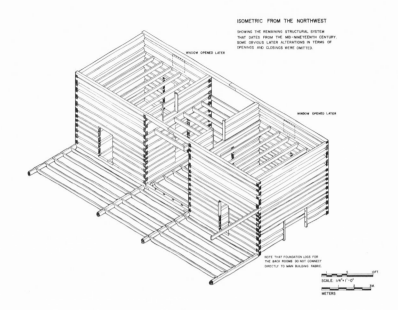

ISOMETRIC FROM THE NORTHWEST

SHOWING THE REMAINING STRUCTURAL SYSTEM
THAT DATES FROM THE MID-NINETEENTH CENTURY.
SOME OBVIOUS LATER ALTERATIONS IN TERMS OF
OPENINGS AND CLOSINGS WERE OMITTED.

WINDOW OPENED LATER

WINDOW OPENED LATER

NOTE THAT FOUNDATION LOGS FOR
THE BACK ROOMS DO NOT CONNECT
DIRECTLY TO MAIN BUILDING FABRIC.

SCALE: 1/4"=1'-0"

METERS

Morehead-Gano Log House, Dallas/Anthony Crosby, Del. 1974

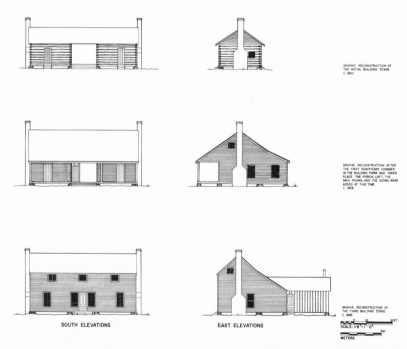

GRAPHIC RECONSTRUCTION AT
THE INITIAL BUILDING STAGE
C. 1850

GRAPHIC RECONSTRUCTION AFTER
THE FIRST SIGNIFICANT CHANGES
IN THE BUILDING FORM HAD TAKEN
PLACE. THE PORCH, LOFT, THE
BACK ROOMS, AND THE SIDING WERE
ADDED AT THIS TIME.
C. 1858

GRAPHIC RECONSTRUCTION AT
THE THIRD BUILDING STAGE.
C. 1895

SOUTH ELEVATIONS

EAST ELEVATIONS

SCALE: 1/8"=1'-0"

METERS

Morehead-Gano Log House/Anthony Crosby, Del. 1974

Morehead-Gano Log House/Dallas County Heritage Society

D'HANIS

Ney, Joseph, House (TEX-3100)
On Parker's Creek 1 mile E. of Farm Road 2200

Stone and stucco, six-bay front, one story, gabled roof, original thatched roof now shingled, rectangular plan, with porch along front; large chimney at east gabled end. Built c. 1850. Two rooms on the west end were added soon after 1850 and used as a store. The builder, Joseph Ney, was a great-nephew of the Napoleonic Marshal, Michel Ney. 3 ext. photos (1936); 1 data page (1936).

DICKENS VICINITY

Matador Half-Dugout (See LUBBOCK, Lubbock County)

Spur-Swenson Granary (See LUBBOCK, Lubbock County)

DRIFTWOOD VICINITY

Johnson's Institute (Camp Ben McCulloch, Friday Mountain Camp) (TEX-398)
6½ miles NE. of Driftwood on Farm Road 1826

Fieldstone, five-bay front, two stories, gabled roof, two-story gallery at rear. Building erected by John Roy, stonemason, in 1852 for Thomas Johnson, a schoolmaster who had come to Texas from Virginia in 1844. There were originally one-room cabins east of the main building to house male students. The school operated for 20 years. Renamed Camp Ben McCulloch, the site was used as a reunion camp for Confederate veterans from 1896 to 1946. It is now the Friday Mountain Boys Camp. 4 ext. photos (1936); 2 data pages (1937).

EL PASO

Hart, Simeon, Grist Mill (TEX-3109)
Gone

Limestone, ruinous in 1936. Built in 1849, this water-powered mill was the first in the area. It not only provided a service to the growers of wheat and corn but also supplied flour to Fort Davis, 200 miles to the east. 1 ext. photo (1936); 1 data page (1936).

FALCON VICINITY

Ramírez, José, House (TEX-3130)
Gone (inundated by Falcon Reservoir)

Stone, 33' x 17'7", one-story, single-room structure with walls 2½' thick, nearly flat roof drained through six "gargolas" of mesquite which penetrated the high parapet. Except for front and rear doors of cyprus, the only openings were small gun ports indicating that this was essentially a fortification. Built in 1781. 4 sheets (1961, including site plan, plans, elevations, sections).

FLORESVILLE VICINITY
Wilson County (247)

Flores, Francisco, Ranch House (TEX-38)
About 7 miles NW. of Floresville

Adobe, rock and brick, four-bay front, one story, hipped roof extends over porch along south and west. Irregular plan. Interior back-to-back fireplaces are small with interesting mantels. A brick wellhouse has a pyramidal brick roof. The adobe and rock portions of the house were begun by Don Francisco Flores in 1844, the brick portions and porches are somewhat later. 4 ext. photos (1936); 1 data page (1936).

Seguin, Juan N., Ranch House (TEX-39)
Gone. Formerly 3 miles N. and ¾ mile W. of Floresville.

Sandstone, stucco and board, 63' x 23', one story, gabled roof, roof extends to cover front porch. Three room linear plan. Walls 22" thick. Built in 1857 by Juan Seguin, cavalry leader in Sam Houston's army at the battle of San Jacinto. 5 sheets (1936, including site plan, plan, elevations, sections, details); 5 ext. photos (1934), 3 ext. photos (1936); 1 data page (1936).

Yndo, Miguel, House (TEX-37)
9 miles NW. of Floresville on Farm Road 1303

Adobe, stone and stucco, one story, gabled roof with lean-to porch across north side. Rectangular plan. Wooden porch columns now replaced with ornamental iron. Built 1855. 4 ext. photos (1936); 1 data page (1936).

FORT DAVIS
Jeff Davis County (122)

Fort Davis (TEX-3102)
1 mile NE. of town of Fort Davis on Tex. 17

National Historic Site. Museum. Fort Davis was established

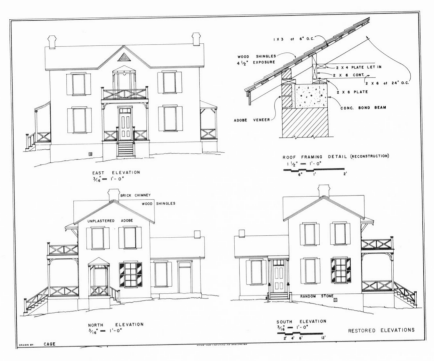

Fort Davis Officers Quarters, Fort Davis/CAGE, Del. 1965

in 1854 and named for Jefferson Davis, then Secretary of War. Its purpose was to end the Indian menace to the routes from San Antonio westward and to honor the Treaty of Guadalupe Hidalgo by cutting off the Apache and Comanche raids into northern Mexico for cattle and horses. The site was strategically questionable, in the narrow canyon of Limpia Creek. Occupied briefly by Confederate troops after the Texas secession, the fort was abandoned from 1862 until 1867. Upon the return of Federal troops, a new fort was constructed where the canyon opens to the plain, a a much less vulnerable position. Some new buildings were of stone, but most of the more than fifty structures were of economical adobe blocks. For 18 years Black troops were stationed at Fort Davis and participated in the engagements which helped to bring the Apaches under control. Official abandonment of the fort came in 1891. Acquisition by the National Park Service was made possible by legislation in

1961. Subsequent restoration and preservation are making Fort Davis a fine example of a typical western fort. 5 ext. photos (1936, including barracks, officers' row, quarters, and chapel) ; 2 data pages (1937). HABSI. NR.

Hospital (TEX-3158). *Main Building*: Adobe, 62'9" (five-bay front) x 46'3", one story, gabled roof; *North and South Wards*: Adobe, 37' x 44'2", one story, gabled roof. Main Building and North Ward were built in 1874-75, the South Ward in 1884-85. 7 sheets (1965, including plans, elevations, sections, details, restored elevations).

Quarters, HB-14 (TEX-3156). Adobe, 40' (three-bay front) x 32'11", two stories, gabled roof, two-story entrance porch. Built 1884-86. 7 sheets (1965, including plans, elevations, details, restored elevations) ; 2 ext. photos (1936).

Magazine (TEX-3159). Volcanic ashlar, 13' square, one story, hipped roof, nail-studded wooden door. 2 sheets (1965, including plan, elevations, detail, and restored elevations).

FORT McKAVETT   Menard County (164)

Fort McKavett (TEX-3111)
22 miles W. of Menard on Farm Road 864

A complex of limestone buildings, mostly one story, including barracks, headquarters building, hospital, schoolhouse, officers' quarters, a two-story commanding officer's house, magazine, guardhouse, bakery, kitchens, feed barns, corrals, and various support facilities, arranged around a central parade ground. Fort McKavett was one of a line of frontier defense posts across Texas which were established about 1851. Abandoned during the Civil War, the fort was re-opened in April 1868 as a cavalry post and a rebuilding program was begun. The hospital was not completed until 1874, only nine years before the last troops were withdrawn and the fort deactivated. Most of the remaining buildings are privately owned, but the schoolhouse and barracks have been restored by the Texas Parks and Wildlife Department as the nucleus of a research and development project encompassing the whole fort. 16 ext. photos (1936, including barracks, headquarters building, commanding officer's house, hospital, and magazine) ; 4 data pages (1937). NR.

FORT WORTH Tarrant County (220)

Pollock-Capps House (TEX-3240)
1120 Penn St.

Roman brick, 54' x 70', two-and-a-half stories, hipped roof with dormers, projecting gables, octagonal corner pavilion with pyramidal roof, one-story front and side porches. Built 1898, attributed to Howard Messer, architect. Remodeled and enlarged, 1910. Good example of Queen Anne design and one of last survivors of a once fashionable residential area. 14 sheets (1972*, including plans, elevations, sections, details). NR.

FREDERICKSBURG Gillespie County (86)

NOTE: All of the following Fredericksburg buildings are listed in the National Register by virtue of being within the boundaries of the Fredericksburg Historic District.

Dietz, Heinrich G., House (TEX-380)
Gone. Formerly Creek Street at Bowie Street.

Limestone, log, board and clapboard, one story, gabled roof with lean-to, attic accessible by outside stair; shed-roofed porch across front. Built in 1848 by Heinrich Gustav Dietz. 4 ext. photos (1936); 1 data page (1937).

First Courthouse (Old Post Office) (TEX-33-A-7)
Gone. Formerly Main Street at Crockett Street.

Ashlar and plaster, 30'10" x 36', two stories, gabled roof, two-story front porch. HABS plans indicate the original design of 1860 had a single room for county offices on the first floor and a courtroom on the second, reached by stairs on the porch. Replaced by present Post Office in 1940. 3 sheets (1934, including site plan, plans, elevations, sections, details); 4 ext. photos (1934); 1 data page (1934).

Kammlah, Heinrich, House (TEX-379)
309 W. Main St.

Museum. Stone, half-timber and stucco, five-bay front, one-

and-a-half stories, gabled, double-pitched roofs, square-post front porch. Built in 1846-50, its rambling plan indicates the multiple functions of store and home. 6 ext. photos (1936) ; 1 data page (1937).

Kiehne-Foerster, House (TEX-381)
405 E. Main St.

Limestone ashlar, three-bay front, two stories, gabled roof, two-story recessed front porch with exterior stair and ornamental wooden railings. Rectangular plan. Walls 24″ thick have some segmental arched openings. Built 1850, it is reputed to be the first two-story house in Fredericksburg. 3 ext. photos (1936) ; 1 data page (1937).

Old Post Office (See *First Courthouse*)

Old St. Mary's Catholic Church (TEX-33-C-2)
San Antonio Street at Orange Street

Limestone, Latin cross plan, 54′4″ x 95′9″ overall, polygonal apse, small transepts, entrance tower 79′ high. Remodeling in 1905 destroyed the original character of the interior, which was made into two floors for a school. Built 1861-63 under the direction of the first priest, Benedictine Father Peter Baunach. Poorly maintained. 4 sheets (1934, including site plan, plan, elevations, sections, details) ; 5 ext. photos (1934) ; 2 data pages (1934).

Pfeil House (TEX-33-A-13)
125 W. San Antonio St.

Stone and stucco, 48′1″ (five-bay front) x 23′1″, two stories, gabled roof, rectangular plan. Segmental-arched window and door openings. Built in the 1840's, it is an example of the domestic architecture of the German colonists; a front porch has been added since 1936. 6 sheets (1934, including site plan, plans, elevations, sections, details) ; 3 ext. photos (1934) ; 1 data page (1934).

Staudt Sunday House (TEX-33-A-8)
512 W. Creek St.

Stone and stucco, 31′9″ (five-bay front) x 22′2″, one story, gabled roof, chimney at each gable end, lesser pitched roof over rear lean-to; greater pitch over front porch which has punch-work and jig-sawn trim. Sunday houses, which may be unique to this area, were built so that families coming the long distances from ranches and farms for the Saturday markets would have a place to stay over for Sunday church-going and social events. Minimal in size, a Sunday house usually had a single room with a loft above, reached by an exterior stair, as at this house. Built by George Geyer, whose original grant for property came from the German Emigration Company in 1847. Enlarged by later owners to four rooms. 2 sheets (1934, including site plan, plan, elevations, section, details); 4 ext. photos (1934); 1 data page (1936).

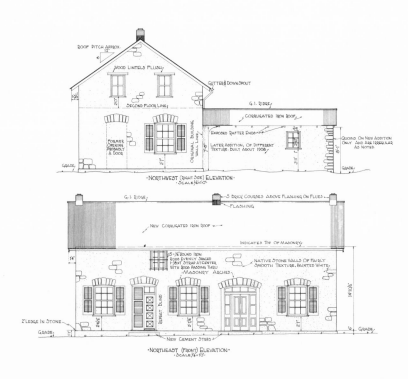

Pfeil House, Fredericksburg/Homer H. Lansberry, Del. 1934

Tatsch, John Peter, House (TEX-33-A-12)
210 N. Bowie St.

Limestone, irregular ashlar, 32'2" (four-bay front) x 29'7", one-and-a-half stories, gabled roof, rear lean-to kitchen with 12'8" stone fireplace chimney and baking oven. Three rooms, walls 2' thick, interior stair to loft. Built 1857 by John Peter Tatsch, who came from Germany in 1852. 2 sheets (1934, including site plan, plan, elevations, section, details) ; 4 ext. photos (1934), 2 ext. photos of former outbuildings (1934) ; 1 data page (1936).

FULTON   Aransas County (4)

Fulton, George W., House (TEX-3116)
S. Beach Street

Cypress siding imitating masonry quoins, shell concrete foundation, reinforced with railroad rails, wall construction of stacked lumber or ties, bolted into place ; three-bay front, three stories and basement, mansard roofs, turrets, and bracketed cornices, round-arched windows in entrance tower. Irregular plan. Victorian interior features marble, ebony, walnut, and imported tile. The bathrooms and central heating system are exceptional for this location and date. Built 1866 for G. W. Fulton, a cousin of Robert Fulton, who came to Texas in the early days of the Republic and married the daughter of Henry Smith, the first provisional governor. The town was named after Fulton. 2 ext. photos (1936) ; 2 data pages (1937). HABSI.

GALVESTON   Galveston County (84)

NOTE: A number of Galveston structures not recorded below have been recorded solely on HABS Inventory forms. They are listed on pages 231-236.

Albert, J. T., House (See *Turner Hall*)

"Ashton Villa" (See *Brown, James Mareau, House*)

Austin, Edward T., House (TEX-261)
1502 Market St. (Ave. D)

Wooden frame, five-bay front, two stories, hipped roof, two-story porch on two sides with rich scrollwork ornament. L-plan. This mansion, incorporating an older house, was built in 1871 of shipped-in mahogany, walnut, and Maine white pine by D. Moffat for Edward T. Austin, a cousin of Stephen F. Austin. 2 ext. photos (1936), 1 int. photo (1936) ; 1 data page (1936). HABSI.

FRONT ELEVATION

NORTH ELEVATION

SOUTH ELEVATION

REAR ELEVATION

George Ball House, Galveston/L. R. Porter, Del. 1936

Ball, George, House (TEX-27)
1405 24th St.

Wood, 29'7" (three-bay front) x 76'3", hipped roof, tetrastyle galleried Doric portico with triglyph and metope frieze. Late Greek Revival detail. This house was on the site of the present Rosenberg Library until 1902 when it was moved and the house divided into two dwellings. What was a former wing is now the house adjacent, on the right. Built about 1857 for George Ball, a silversmith, jeweler, and merchant originally from New York City. 7 sheets (1936, including site plan, plans, elevations, sections, details) ; 2 ext. photos (1936), 2 int. photos (1936) ; 1 data page (1936), 3 data pages (1967). HABSI.

"Bishop's Palace" (See *Gresham, Colonel Walter, House*)

Brown-Denison-Moore House (Bartlett Moore House) (TEX-257)
Gone. Formerly 3112 Ave. O.

Wooden frame with clapboarding, five-bay front, two stories, hipped roof, tetrastyle Doric portico with delicate railed second-story balcony, elliptical fan light over front door. Greek Revival detail. Built c. 1858 by Guy M. Brown, an early Galveston shipper, later owned by Colonel Denison and Bartlett Moore. 2 ext. photos (1936) ; 1 data page (1936).

Brown, James Mareau, House ("Ashton Villa," El Mina Shrine Temple) (TEX-33-B-3)
2328 Broadway

Brick, 48'10" (five-bay front) x 53', three stories, hipped roof with deep projecting eaves supported by large, paired brackets. Polygonal bay wing at right. Two-story 77' x 35' kitchen and stable at rear, gabled roof, Italianate detail. A palatial residence with large, high-ceilinged rooms, richly ornamented by French artisans with decorative plaster, 22-carat gold leaf, carved walnut, and red tile. Built 1858-59. Col. James M. Brown, a master of the brick mason's trade from an early apprenticeship in New York and along the Ohio River, was his own architect and builder, and the brick used was burned in his own brickyard. Experienced as a contractor, he was also a successful hardware merchant and banker. Since 1928 the building has been the El Mina Shrine Temple. 8 sheets (1934, including site plan, plans, elevations, sections, and details of house and stables) ; 7 ext. photos (1934), 2 ext. photos (1936), 3 int. photos (1934), 3 int. photos (1936), 1 ext. photo (1967*), 2 int. photos (1967*) ; 3 data pages (1936), 3 data pages (1967*). HABSI. NR.

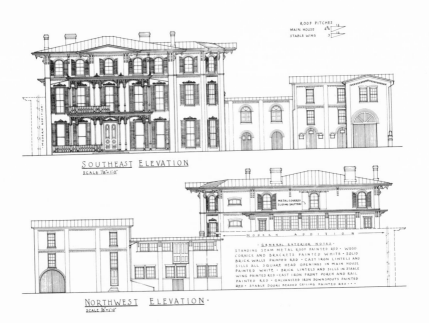

James Mareau Brown House, Galveston/James I. Campbell, Del. 1934

Cherry, Wilbur F., House (TEX-252)
1602 Church St. (Ave. F)

Wooden frame with clapboarding, 20' (five-bay front) x 36', exclusive of rear additions, two stories, gabled roof, chimney at each gable end, two-story gallery with square wooden columns. Center-hall plan. Modest Greek Revival detail. Built c. 1852-54, it survived an 1885 fire which destroyed most of the forty-block surrounding area. 1 ext. photo (1936), 1 ext. photo (1967*) ; 1 data page (1936), 3 data pages (1967*) ; HABSI.

Darragh, Mrs. John L., House (TEX-2104)
519 15th St.

Wooden frame, 47' x 58', two stories with raised basement, hipped roofs, two-story gallery across front terminated at octagonal tower at right; elliptical foundation arches are brick, stuccoed to resemble stone. The iron fence is especially elaborate and noteworthy. Built 1888. Architect, Alfred Muller; builder, R. Zinke. Two older houses were incorporated in the construction. 3 ext. photos (1967*), 1 int. photo (1967*) ; 3 data pages (1967*) ; HABSI.

Eaton Memorial Chapel of Trinity Episcopal Church (See also *Trinity Episcopal Church* (TEX-295)
710 22nd St.

Brick, stuccoed to resemble stone, 45' (five-bay front) x 85', two stories, hipped roof with gabled projections, buttresses have pinnacles projecting above the cornice, lancet windows. Gothic Revival detail. The principal interior space fills the second floor where the paneled ceiling is divided by massive intersecting beams having ornate plaster pendants. Built 1878-81. The project had been envisioned by, and named for, Benjamin Eaton, who came from Ireland and Missouri to Galveston in 1841, and organized Trinity parish, which he served as rector until his death in 1871. The architects were Clayton and Lynch. 1 ext. photo (1967*), 1 int. photo (1967*) ; 4 data pages (1967*) ; HABSI.

El Mina Shrine Temple (See *Brown, James Mareau, House*)

Federal Building (See *U. S. Custom House*)

First Presbyterian Church, Galveston/Allen Stross, Photo 1967

First Presbyterian Church (TEX-2106)
Church and 19th Streets

Brick, stuccoed to resemble limestone, 60′ x 128′6″, gabled facade flanked by towers, one having steep pyramidal roof. Semicircular window and door arches. Construction begun 1872; chapel and Sunday School portion completed 1876; finished and dedicated February 1889. Plans and specifications by Jones and Baldwin of Memphis, Tennessee, whose field supervisor, Nicholas Clayton, stayed in Galveston after the completion of the church to establish his own practice. 8 ext. photos (1967*), 3 int. photos (1967*); 10 data sheets (1967*).

Galveston Bagging and Cordage Company Factory (TEX-153)

Gone. Formerly Winnie Street between 38th and 39th.

Brick, 260' x 300', one story, hipped roof, with one three-story tower at center and one at each end of the principal facade. The towers contained water tanks with a combined capacity of 20,000 gallons to supply a fire-protection sprinkler system. Circular stairs in each of the end towers. The trussed-span interior provided space for 100 machines under a single foreman. The only such bagging mill in Texas, it was constructed in 1888 to break a New England monopoly on jute. The factory was closed in 1896. 5 sheets (1967*, including site plan, plans, elevations, section) ; 1 ext. photo (1967*), 1 int. photo (1967*) ; 5 data pages (1967*) ; HABSI.

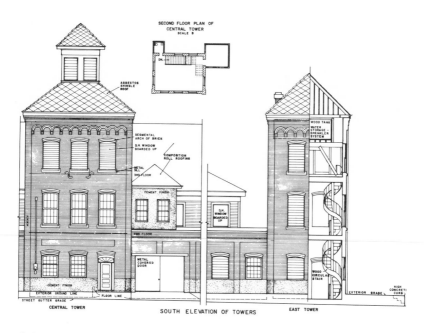

Galveston Bagging and Cordage Company Factory, Galveston/ Michael Casey, Del. 1967

Galveston News Building (TEX-289)
Gone. Formerly 2108 Mechanic St.

Pressed brick, 50' x 120', three stories, elaborately detailed facade, an arrangement of pilasters and arches in red, cream, gray, and black brick, and tile. Designed by Nicholas Clayton, built in 1883-84. Founded in 1842, the Galveston *News* is Texas' oldest newspaper and occupied this building for 80 years. 1 int. photo (1967*) ; 3 data pages (1967*).

Colonel Walter Gresham House ("The Bishop's Palace"), Galveston/
Allen Stross, Photo 1967

SOUTH ELEVATION

Gresham House/Larry D. Johnston, Del. 1967

Gresham, Colonel Walter, House ("The Bishop's Palace")
(TEX-2103)
1402 Broadway

Museum. Rock-faced Texas pink granite with sculptured limestone and red sandstone trim, 88′ x 104′ overall, three stories above high basement, elaborate tile roof with hips, gables, cones and pyramids corresponding to the articulation of the complex asymmetrical plan, delicate ironwork railings at balconies and verandas. An octagonal stairwell with stained glass windows rises from the central interior space; large, richly decorated main hall, library, semicircular conservatory, dining room, and two parlors are arranged around it. The kitchen was a model of up-to-date achievement in its period. Commissioned by Gresham upon his election to the United States Congress in September 1887, it was designed by architect Nicholas J. Clayton and built in 1887-93. From 1923 until the early 1960's the Gresham house was the official residence of the Bishop of the Roman Catholic Diocese of Galveston. 11 sheets (1967*, including site plan, plans, elevations, section, details) ; 3 ext. photos (1967*), 9 int. photos (1967*) ; 5 data pages (1967*) ; HABSI. NR.

Gresham House/Allen Stross, Photo 1967

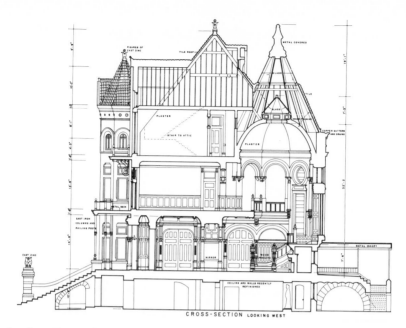

Gresham House/James E. Murphy, Del. 1967

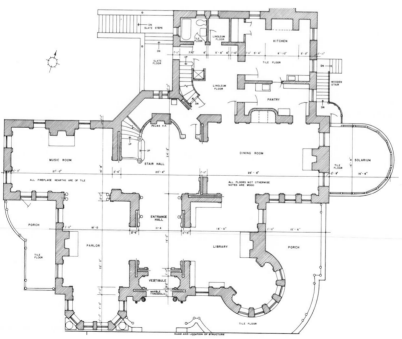

Gresham House/James E. Murphy and Gerald R. Rapp, Del. 1967

Grover, George W., House (TEX-296)
1520 Market St.

Brick with stucco quoins, 30' (three-bay front) x 80', two stories, hipped roof, two story front gallery with three square columns. Side hall plan. Built 1859 of locally burned brick. George Washington Grover was an Indian fighter, Texas pioneer, Mexican prisoner, gold prospector, and Civil War mayor of Galveston. 3 ext. photos (1967*), 1 int. photo (1967*) ; 4 data pages (1967*) ; HABSI.

"Heidenheimer Castle" (See *Sydnor-Heidenheimer House*)

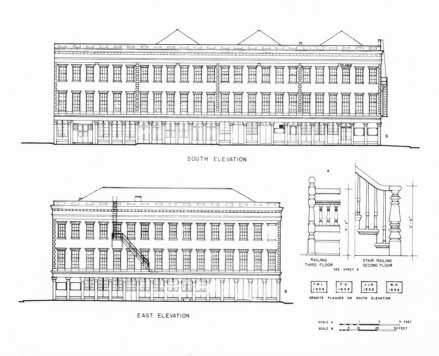

SOUTH ELEVATION

EAST ELEVATION

Hendley Building, Galveston/Michael Casey, Del. 1967

Hendley Building (TEX-290)
2000-2016 Strand

Brick with granite, 94' x 50', gabled roof, three stories, an entire block divided by fire walls into four units separated on the facade by granite quoins, square Maine granite piers at the ground floor level, low gables concealed by parapet. The upper stories have offices arranged around skylighted wells. Windows have louvered interior shutters. Built by the shipping firm of William Hendley and Company (William and Joseph Hendley with John Sleight) in 1855-58 in the commercial center of Galveston, importing brick, granite, and other building materials from Boston. During the Civil War this building was a Confederate watch tower, and from a wooden cupola on the roof eight master mariners and ships' captains kept watch over the shipping in the Gulf of Mexico. After the war the space was returned to the offices of commission merchants, cotton buyers, attorneys, and shipping agents. 7 sheets (1967*, including site plan, plans, elevation, details, section) ; 2 ext. photos (1967*), 1 int. photo (1967*) ; 3 data pages (1967*) ; HABSI. In NR by being within boundaries of "The Strand" Historic District.

Hutchings, John H., House (TEX-154)
2816 Ave. O

Brick, stuccoed, gabled roof, three stories; one-story portico on south and west intersects two-story pedimented portico on west. Center-hall plan. Curvilinear bays and decorative brickwork; gabled roof largely concealed by flush cornice. Neo-Renaissance detail. Built for John Henry Hutchings, c. 1859, a prominent banker and shipper, and his bride, by her uncle and guardian, Robert Mills. Enlarged by the design of Nicholas Clayton about 1891. Carriage house has round, flat-roofed decorated tower, arches, and doorway. 3 ext. photos of main house (1967*), 1 ext. photo of carriage house (1967*), 3 int. photos (1967*) ; 5 data pages (1967*) ; HABSI.

Landes, Henry A., House (TEX-2102)
1604 Post Office St.

Museum. Pressed brick, 69' x 60' overall, two-and-a-half stories, hipped roof with slate shingles intersected by gable and tower forms. This house is symmetrical about a diagonal axis, the southeast corner facade is flanked by octagonal towers, capped by a strange, square-topped gable and encircled by a two-story veranda of delicate ironwork. Center-hall plan. Heavy late 19th-century detail. Built 1886-87. Architect George E. Dickey designed the house for Kentucky-born Henry A. Landes, whose family settled in Texas in 1851. Landes became a member of the mercantile firm of Wallis, Landes & Co., as well as wholesale grocer, cotton factor, liquor dealer, importer, real estate investor, and director of banking and loan businesses. 2 ext. photos (1967*), 1 int. photo (1967*) ; 3 data pages (1967*); HABSI.

Lasker, Morris, House (TEX-2100)
Gone. Formerly in 1700 block of Broadway.

Stuccoed brick, 60′ x 75′ overall dimensions, two stories, steep hipped roof of slate with dormers, gabled projections, circular and octagonal bays, decorated pilasters, and a double-tiered porch with delicate ironwork. Asymmetrical plan with first-floor rooms connected by large double sliding doors. Nicholas Clayton, architect. Built 1889-91 by August W. Bautsch for Prussian-born Morris Lasker, wealthy Galveston businessman and philanthropist. 4 ext. photos (1967*), 3 int. photos (1967*) ; 4 data pages (1967*).

Lewis, Allen, House (TEX-256)
Gone. Formerly 2328 Ave. G.

Wooden frame with clapboarding, three-bay front, two stories, gabled roof, giant pedimented Doric portico and square pilasters. L-plan. Greek Revival detail. Elegant interior stair. Built at Avenue J and 25th Street in the 1840's, moved in 1870 to Avenue G. 2 ext. photos (1936), 1 int. photo (1936) ; 1 data page (1936).

Marwitz, Herman, House (TEX-2105)
Gone. Formerly 801 22nd St.

Brick and stone, three stories, gabled and mansard roofs, elliptical arcaded porch with circular corner pavilion at

Herman Marwitz House, Galveston/Allen Stross, Photo 1967

"piano nobile" entrance level reached by monumental curving stair. Rich Victorian detail. Built 1890-94. Architect, Alfred Muller. From 1895 to 1900 it housed the Goldbeck College, a private school. 2 ext. photos (1967*) ; HABSI.

Medical School, University of Texas (TEX-292)
914-916 Strand

Red brick, 200′ x 70′, 102′-high central pavilion, simple hipped roof replaces pagoda-like roof destroyed by hurricane in 1900. Columned arcades, with giant order for the two lower stories and a diminutive scale at the third story. Richardson Romanesque detail. Interior includes large instruc-

Medical School, Galveston/Allen Stross, Photo 1967

tional amphitheatres. Built 1888-91. Architect Nicholas
Clayton, who visited Medical Schools in Baltimore, Philadelphia, New York, and Boston before preparing his plans. 3
ext. photos (1967*), 3 int. photos (1967*); 4 data pages
(1967*); HABSI. NR.

Menard, Michel B., House (TEX-26)
1603 33rd St.

Wooden frame with clapboarding, 26′ x 64′, two stories, plus
one-story south wing and two-story north wing, hipped roof,
Ionic tetrastyle portico with matching shallower porches at
wings. Greek Revival. Built c. 1839; altered 1843. Canada-

born Michel Menard was the founder of the Galveston City Company which, in 1837, began the survey and sale of town lots for the new city. 5 sheets (1936, including plans, elevations, section, details) ; 3 ext. photos (1936), 2 ext. photos (1967*), 2 int. photos (1967*) ; 1 data page (1936), 4 data pages (1967*) ; HABSI.

Moody, M. L., House (TEX-254)
Gone. Formerly at Ave. M and 23rd St.

Brick, seven-bay front, three stories, flat roof, two-story Doric-columned entrance portico; square-columned two- and three-deck gallery in rear ell; five-bay, semicircular conservatory. Built 1859-60 for Thomas M. League. After the Civil War it became a fashionable boarding house, later the home of M. L. Moody. It was used in the 1930's as a Catholic high school. 2 ext. photos (1936) ; 1 data page (1936).

M. L. Moody House, Galveston/Harry Starnes, Photo 1936

Moore, Bartlett, House (See *Brown-Denison-Moore House*)

Powhatan House (TEX-28)
3427 Ave. O

Museum.Wooden frame with clapboarding, 45'2" x 39'7", flat roof, three-column Doric portico, ornamental iron balcony over entrance. Greek Revival detail. Built 1847 by Mayor John S. Sydnor at a location bounded by 21st and 22nd Streets and Avenues M and N. As early as 1852 it was operated as the "Powhatan House," a hotel. After a variety of occupancies the house was bought in 1881 by the city of Galveston and used to house an orphanage until 1893. Under new ownership it was then divided into three parts, moved to sites between 34th and 35th Streets, and each part remodeled into a separate house. This third of the original building which has survived bears evidence of several different periods of construction. 7 sheets (1936, including plans, elevations, sections, details); 2 ext. photos (1936), 1 int. photo (1936), 2 ext. photos (1967*), 2 int. photos (1967*); 1 data page (1936), 5 data pages (1967*).

Rosenberg, Henry, House (TEX-260)
1306 Market St. (Ave. D)

Brick, stuccoed, 42'5" (five-bay front) x 91', two stories, hipped roof with cupola, bracketed eaves, one-story entrance portico, decorated gallery at rear; attached kitchen. Much of the Greek Revival and Italianate detail of this transitional house has been removed in converting it into apartments. Built 1859 for Henry Rosenberg, whose philanthropies have continued to serve Galveston since his death in 1893. A carriage house, given by Mrs. Rosenberg as a club house for the United Daughters of the Confederacy, is now also divided into apartments. 5 sheets (1967*, including site plan, plans, elevations, details), 1 sheet (n.d., showing drawing for the Rosenberg Library, shows also a cupola on the house, and balconies not present in other drawings); 2 ext. photos (1936), 2 ext. photos (1937), 2 ext. photos (1967*), 2 int. photos (1967*); 1 data page (1936), 4 data pages (1967*); HABSI.

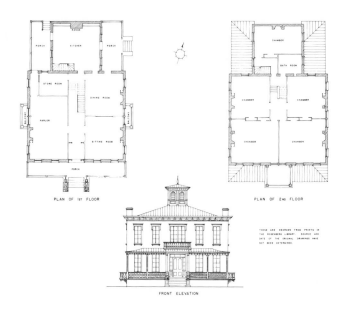

PLAN OF 1st FLOOR   PLAN OF 2nd FLOOR

FRONT ELEVATION

Henry Rosenberg House, Galveston/Gerald R. Rapp, Del. 1967

Rosenberg House/Harry Starnes, Photo 1937

111

St. Mary's Cathedral (TEX-293)
21st Street and Church Avenue

Stuccoed brick, Latin cross plan, gabled roof, Gothic Revival detail. Begun in 1847 under French-born John May Odin, first Bishop of Galveston, with a gift of 500,000 bricks from Belgium. In 1876 Nicholas Clayton designed the transept tower; in 1884 he supervised the heightening of the two front towers, which were later repaired in 1900 following a hurricane, and again remodeled in 1907. 7 sheets (1967*, including site plan, plans, elevations, sections, details) ; 1 ext. photo (1967*), 1 int. photo (1967*) ; 2 data pages (1967*). NR.

Sealy, George, House (TEX-298)
2424 Broadway

Roman brick, 70′ x 80′, two-and-a-half stories, steep hipped tile roof with dormers. Open arcade across front at first floor, clustered chimneys. A central paneled hall has a beamed ceiling and oak stair, the library is finished in cherry, the drawing room has white mouldings surrounding panels of yellow silk and the dining room wainscot is paneled in mahogany. Attributed to Stanford White of McKim, Mead and White, built 1889-91. The supervising architect, Nicholas Clayton, designed the brick stables. Pennsylvania-born George Sealy came to Galveston in 1857 and achieved success in the banking and loan business, in railroads, stock market, manufacturing, publishing, and import-export trade. 2 ext. photos (1967*), 4 int. photos (1967*), 2 ext. photos of stable and carriage house (1967*) ; 5 data pages (1967*) ; HABSI. NR.

Sydnor-Heidenheimer House ("Heidenheimer Castle") (TEX-2101)
1602 Sealy Ave.

Stuccoed brick and tabby concrete with oyster shell aggregate, 30′ (three-bay front) x 40′, two-and-a-half stories above raised basement, hipped roof with dormers at front, mansard and flat roofs at rear, masonry entrance porch with pointed arches, squared pillars, and flight of steps. Added ell, 24′ x 50′. An octagonal tower marks the junction of the older and new parts of the structure, and a roofless arcade ornaments the 16th Street side. Decorative paneling and archway in interior. Built 1855 by Colonel John S. Sydnor, mayor of Galveston in the 1850's. Sold about 1888 to Sampson Heidenheimer, early Galveston merchant and auctioneer, who spent $15,000 enlarging and remodeling the house according to designs of Nicholas Clayton, producing a medieval effect. 3 ext. photos (1967*), 1 int. photo (1967*) ; 3 data pages (1967*) ; HABSI.

Trinity Episcopal Church (See also *Eaton Memorial Chapel*) (TEX-294)
708 22nd St.

Brick, 63'6" x 123', gabled roof, with central entrance tower, eight side bays marked by exterior buttresses and interior hammer-beam trusses. Lancet window openings. Interior cluster columns define the side aisles. The congregation of Trinity Episcopal Church was organized in 1841 under the leadership of the Reverend Benjamin Eaton. The small frame structure which first served the parish was replaced by the present building in 1857. Architect, John De Young; granite and brickwork by Frank Brown. In 1925 the building was raised 4'6" by hand-operated jacks. 7 sheets (1967*, including site plan, plans, elevations, sections) ; 3 ext. photos (1967*), 2 int. photos (1967*) ; 6 data pages (1967*).

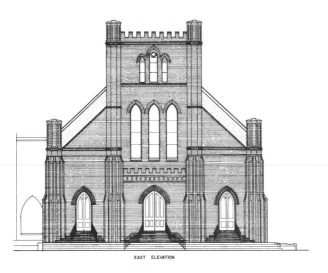

EAST ELEVATION

Trinity Episcopal Church, Galveston/Michael Casey, Del. 1967

Trube, John C., House (TEX-299)
1621-1627 Sealy Ave.

Brick stuccoed, two-and-a-half stories with "piano nobile," slate-shingled mansard roof with elaborate dormers. Irregular plan. Entrance steps rise diagonally to a quarter-circle Ionic porch. Every exterior surface is ornamented with exuberant detail. Built 1890. Alfred Muller, architect; John W. Pope, builder. 2 ext. photos (1967*), 1 int. photo (1967*); 3 data pages (1967*).

Trueheart-Adriance Building (TEX-291)
212 22nd St. (Kempner St.)

Pressed brick, three stories, 26' x 42'. The facade is ornamented with paneled brickwork pilasters, cast iron columns and caps, heavily bracketed cornice and pedimented parapet flanked by acroteria. Polychrome brickwork, long concealed by paint now restored. Built 1881. Nicholas Clayton, architect. 5 sheets (1967, including plans, elevations, sections); 3 ext. photos (1967*), 1 int. photo (1967*); 4 data pages (1967*); HABSI. NR.

Turner Hall (J. T. Albert House) (TEX-21)
Gone. Originally 2015 Ave. I.

Wooden frame, block siding, 40'10" (five-bay front) x 20'1", two stories, hipped roof, galleried two-story Doric portico. Greek Revival detail. Built 1858 by a Turnverein Lodge of German immigrants. Membership growth by 1880 required an addition to accommodate dances and theatricals. 4 sheets (1934, including plans, elevations, sections, details); 8 ext. photos (1934), 2 ext. photos (1936), 1 int. photo (1936); 1 data page (1936).

U. S. Custom House (Federal Building) (TEX-259)
20th and Post Office Streets

Brick, 80' (five-bay front) x 106', two stories, hipped roof, recessed porticos centered in long facades, projecting portico on west facade, columns of cast iron, Ionic at the first story, Corinthian at second story. A three-story design by architect Ammi B. Young was the originally accepted plan in 1857, but the building by Cluskey and Moore, contracted by Blan-

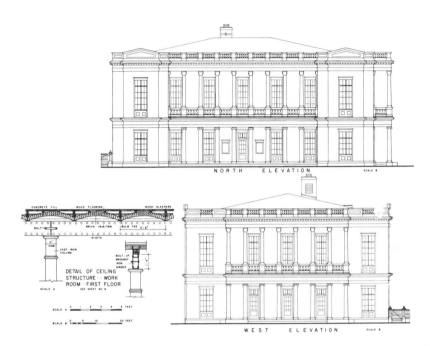

U.S. Custom House, Galveston/Larry D. Johnston and
Gerald R. Rapp, Del. 1967

dell and Emerson of Boston, and completed in 1861, is of a
different design. Changes were made during the Civil War
and repairs in 1865, and further renovations later in the
19th century. 8 sheets (1967*, including site plan, plans,
elevations, section); 1 ext. photo (1936), 4 ext. photos
(1967*), 1 int. photo (1967*); 1 data page (1936), 5 data
pages (1967*); HABSI. NR.

Ursuline Convent (TEX-3227)
Avenue N and 25th Street

Stuccoed brick, painted white, approx. 140′ x 90′, three-and-
a-half stories, gabled roof with modified Palladian dormers.
Rectangular shuttered windows under segmental masonry
arches. Seven Ursuline nuns from New Orleans came to Galveston in 1847 to establish a convent and an academy for

girls. In 1858 a long rectangular nunnery was built and in 1860 a square building of similar size was added at the east as a dormitory and classroom building, giving the completed building a T-plan. During the Civil War the nuns operated these buildings as a hospital. 2 ext. photos (1967*) ; HABSI.

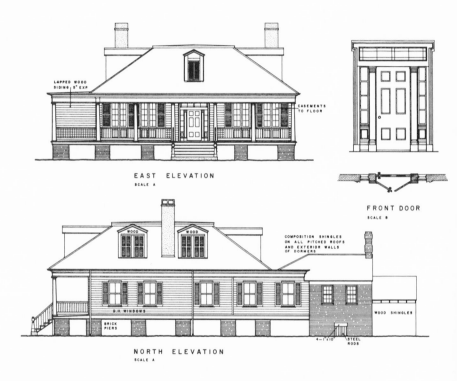

EAST ELEVATION
SCALE A

FRONT DOOR
SCALE B

NORTH ELEVATION
SCALE A

Williams-Tucker House, Galveston/James E. Murphy, Del. 1967

Williams-Tucker House (TEX-297)
3601 Ave. P

Museum. Wooden frame with clapboarding, 50′ (five-bay front) x 56′, one-and-a-half stories, hipped roof with gabled dormers and a flat deck, once the floor of a cupola which burned in 1890. A wide columned gallery extends across the front and one side; an ell extension on north side connects with the old brick kitchen. Before the grade-raising of 1905 there was a ground floor, and the principal floor was a "piano nobile." A central hall contains a graceful stair with a split landing. Samuel May Williams, for whom the house was built in 1849-51, was a native of Rhode Island who came to Texas in 1822 and was for 11 years land agent for the Austin colony. In later years Williams advanced large sums of money to the destitute Texas government and provided many banking functions in the absence of a bank of Texas. With his death in 1855 the property was sold to his friend Phillip Tucker. 6 sheets (1967*, including site plan, plans, elevations, sections, details) ; 3 ext. photos (1967*), 2 int. photos (1967*) ; 7 data pages (1967*) ; HABSI. NR.

Wolston, John, House (TEX-258)
Gone. Formerly 1705 35th St.

Wooden frame, three-bay front, two stories, hipped roof, giant tetrastyle Doric portico. Greek Revival detail. Built in 1859 by John Wolston, an early cotton merchant in Galveston. Lumber came from Louisiana by schooner, and the house was built by slave labor. 1 ext. photo (1936) ; 1 data page (1936).

GENEVA VICINITY   Sabine County (202)

Ybarbo Ranch House (See NACOGDOCHES AND VICINITY, Nacogdoches County)

GOLIAD AND VICINITY   Goliad County (88)

La Bahia Presidio Chapel (TEX-387)
2 miles S. on U.S. 183

National Historic Site. Museum. Stone, barrel-vaulted with octagonal window openings, a square belfry rises above the baptistry at the left of the arched entrance. Although the chapel has remained standing through nearly two centuries, the surrounding fort was reconstructed in the 1960's. Presidio Nuestra Señora de Loreto de la Bahia was established at its present site in 1749 as a military post to protect the Franciscan mission of Espiritu Santo de Zuñiga established at the same time on the opposite side of the San Antonio River. The stone chapel and other stone buildings were built

La Bahia Presidio Chapel, Goliad/Richard MacAllister, Photo 1936

after 1765. After the missions under its protection were abandoned the Presidio La Bahia remained a military post, important in wars for Mexican independence from Spain and Texas independence from Mexico. In March 1836, Col. James Fannin, defeated in the battle of Coleto, was shot, with more than 300 of his men, after a week's imprisonment in the chapel. Their massacre made "Remember Goliad" a rallying cry of the Texas Revolution. 5 ext. photos (1936); 1 data page (1936). NR.

Boyd, William H., House (TEX-303)
Gone.

Limestone and stucco, two stories, gabled roof. Outside stairs removed in 1858 and rebuilt inside. Center-hall plan. Built c. 1846 as a drugstore and printshop, it was bought by William H. Boyd in the 1860's and partitioned to house his large family. There is also a small attached stone ell. 3 ext. photos (1936); 1 data page (1937).

Davis House (TEX-385)
Gone.

Stone and stucco, three-bay front, one-and-a-half stories remodeled to two stories after partial destruction by a tornado in 1903; hipped roof. Built 1855 by John S. McCampbell. 4 ext. photos (1936); 1 data page (1937).

Peck, Captain Barton, House (TEX-384)
W. edge of Goliad, 2 blocks S. of U.S. 59

Stone and stucco, three-bay front, two stories and basement, hipped roof and gabled, two-story portico, quoined corners, gabled rear wing, half stone and half wooden frame with clapboarding. Center hall plan. Curved stair probably later than 1848-52 construction. 5 ext. photos (1936), 3 int. photos (1936), 3 ext. photos of outbuildings (separate rubble stone and plaster kitchen with large central chimney) (1936); 1 data page (1937).

HEMPSTEAD VICINITY   Waller County (237)

"Liendo" (TEX-33-B-4)
4 miles E. of Hempstead via Farm Road 1488, Wyatt Chapel Road and private road.

Wooden frame, two stories, 56' (five-bay front) x 69', hipped roof, with pedimented, two-story portico having four square columns. L-plan. Greek Revival detail. Built in 1853 as the plantation house of Leonard Croce. The house and 1100 acres of land were purchased in 1873 by the sculptress Elisabet Ney and her husband, Dr. Edmund Montgomery. 5 sheets (1934, including illustrated condensed data, site plan, plans, elevations, sections, details); 5 ext. photos (1934), 2 ext. photos (1936), 1 int. photo (1936); 3 data pages (1936). NR.

HILLSBORO   Hill County (109)

Hill County Courthouse (TEX-138)
Public Square - Waco, Covington and Franklin Streets

Limestone, rock-faced, 92'6" square, three stories, gabled

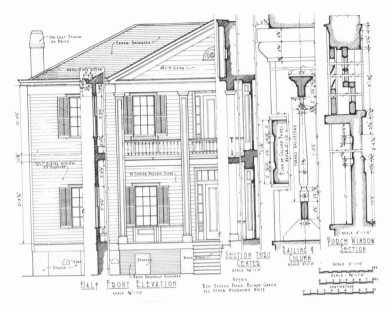

Liendo Plantation, Hempstead Vicinity/Arthur E. Hutter, Del. 1934

Hill County Courthouse, Hillsboro/W. Eugene George, Photo 1961

entrance pavilions at each side and mansarded corner pavilions, richly carved pilasters, entrance arches, and window trim. Symmetrical plan. The central, three-stage clock tower is typical of the designs of W. C. Dodson, a Waco architect who designed at least a dozen Texas courthouses. The $83,000 contract was awarded to Lovell, Miller, and Hood in December 1889, and the courthouse accepted as complete in September 1891. 5 ext. photos (1961); 4 data pages (1961). HABSI. NR.

HOUSTON   Harris County (101)

Carrington, Dr., House (TEX-33-B-2)
Gone. Formerly at Crawford Street and Rusk Avenue

Brick, 37'8" (three-bay front) x 54'11", two stories, hipped roof, two-story front porch with ornamental wood balustrade at upper level. Built in 1851 for D. B. Botts, a relative of Dr. Carrington, with a brick addition 1868, frame addition 1885. 4 sheets (1934, including site plan, plans, elevations, sections, details); 5 ext. photos (1934), 3 ext. photos (1936), 1 int. photo (1936); 1 data page (1936).

Cherry House (See Nichols-Rice-Cherry House)

Kellum-Noble House (Shelter House) (TEX-23)
Sam Houston Park, 212 Dallas Ave.

Museum. Brick, 56'11" (five-bay front) x 64'9", two stories, hipped roof, L-plan, encircling two-story gallery, brick piers below, wooden posts and railing above, exterior stair only. Interior partitions also of brick. Built 1847 by Nathaniel K. Kellum, who operated a brick kiln. In the 1850's Mrs. Zerviah M. Noble conducted a private school in the house. Acquired by the city with the surrounding grounds in 1899, it became part of Sam Houston Park and was used as museum, caretaker's residence, and shelter house at various times. It was opened to visitors in 1956 after being restored by the Harris County Heritage Society. 4 sheets (1936, including site plan, plans, elevations, sections, details); 2 ext. photos (1936); 1 data page (1936). HABSI.

Kellum-Noble House (Shelter House), Houston/
Woodlief F. Brown, Del. 1936

Longcope, E., House (TEX-22)
Gone. Formerly 102 Chenevert St.

Brick and stucco with painted quoins and arches, 40'3" (five-bay front) x 30'1", two stories, flat roof, ornamental iron gallery across front. Built 1845. 3 sheets (1934, including site plan, plans, elevations, sections, details); 5 ext. photos (1934), 2 ext. photos (1936); 1 data page (1936).

Nichols-Rice-Cherry House (TEX 33-B-1)
Sam Houston Park (Built at 300 block San Jacinto Street; moved to San Jacinto and Franklin Streets, 1873; moved to 608 Fargo Ave., 1896; moved to Sam Houston Park after 1959)

Museum. Wooden frame with clapboarding, 39'5" (three-bay front) x 50', two stories, truncated hip roof of terne metal with widow's walk, two-story portico with four Ionic columns at each level. Greek Revival. Built c. 1850, by Ebenezer B. Nichols, a native of Cooperstown, N. Y., who sold it in 1851 to his business partner, William Marsh Rice, the founder of Rice University. Other owners between 1863 and 1897 placed a gabled roof over the original roof. In 1897 a bid of $25 for the entranceway, with its notable anthemion-banded cornice, was the only offer for the entire house. It then became the property of Mrs. E. Richardson Cherry, who moved it to Fargo Avenue. Since 1959 the house has been moved again and restored by the Harris County Heritage Society. 4 sheets (1934, including plans, elevations which show original roof-lines, sections, details) ; 5 ext. photos (1934), 3 ext. photos (1936), 2 int. photos (1936) ; 1 data page (1936). HABSI.

Shelter House (See *Kellum-Noble House*)

HUNTSVILLE VICINITY   Walker County (236)

Yoakum, Henderson, House (TEX-231)
Gone.

Wood, one-and-a-half stories, gabled roof with narrow gabled dormer over front entrance. Built 1850 for Henderson Yoakum, pioneer Texas historian. 1 ext. photo (1936) ; 1 data page (1936).

INDEPENDENCE AND VICINITY
Washington County (239)

Baptist Church (TEX-29)
Farm Road 390 at Farm Road 50

Stone, gabled roof, built 1872 for a congregation organized in 1839. 1 ext. photo (1936), 1 int. photo (1936) ; 1 data page (1936).

Clark House (See *Holmes, Willet, House*)

Holmes, Willet, House (Clark House) (TEX-211)
Gone.

Wooden frame, two stories, gabled roof, two-story gallery

across front, brick chimney at each gable end. Built 1840.
2 ext. photos (1936).

Houston, Mrs. Sam, House (TEX-264)
Farm Road 390, 0.1 mile E. of Farm Road 50

Wooden frame, gabled roof, two stories with two-story entrance porch. Built by Isaac Root in 1848. Site of Mrs. Houston's death in 1867. 1 ext. photo (1936); 1 data page (1937). NR.

Mexican Jail (Toalson House) (TEX-263)
One-half block S. of Farm Road 390, 2 blocks E. of Farm
   Road 50

Adobe, gabled roof, one story, porch across front. Built 1834 or 1835, later altered. 2 ext. photos (1936); 1 data page (1936).

Robertson, General Jerome B., House (TEX-33-B-9)
One block S. and E. of intersection of Farm Roads 50 and 390

Wooden frame with clapboarding, 47'4" x 38', one story, gabled roof, stone chimney at each gable end. Built between 1845 and 1849. General Jerome Bonaparte Robertson came to Texas from Kentucky. He and his son were both generals in the Confederate Army. 2 sheets (1934, including site plan, plan, elevations, sections, details); 4 ext photos (1934), 2 ext. photos (1936); 1 data page (1936).

Seward, John H., House (TEX-33-B-8)
One mile E. of Independence on Farm Road 390

Wooden frame (cedar), 72'3" (five-bay front) x 43'9", two stories, gabled roof, two-story porch along full length of front and portion of side, later one-story additions at rear. Built 1855. Moved ¾ mile east in 1856. 4 sheets (1934, including site plan, plans, elevations, sections, details); 4 ext. photos (1934), 3 ext. photos (1936); 1 data page (1936).

Seward, Samuel, House (TEX-262)
2 miles NE. of Independence

Wooden frame with clapboarding, gabled roof, two-story

John H. Seward House, Independence Vicinity/ Harry Starnes, Photo 1936

veranda. Built in 1827 for Samuel Seward, a planter from Virginia. 1 ext. photo (1936); 1 data page (1936).

Toalson House (See *Mexican Jail*)

ITASCA VICINITY   Hill County (109)

Randle-Turner House (TEX-136)
8 miles SE. of Itasca on Farm Road 934

Wooden frame, mortised and pegged, with cypress siding, 50′2″ (seven-bay front) x 48′4″, one story, gabled roof, dogtrot plan with porch along south side, chimney at each gable end. Oldest portions built by "Old Man" Randle on the northern frontier of the Republic of Texas before 1845. Abandoned after 1951. 5 sheets (1961, including site plan, plans, elevations, section); 8 ext. photos (1961); 4 data pages (1962).

JEFFERSON AND VICINITY   Marion County (158)

NOTE: The majority of the Jefferson buildings recorded by HABS are included in the National Register by virtue of being within the boundaries of the Jefferson Historic District. Those also listed as separate entries are noted below.

Abernathy-Singleton House (TEX-146)
204 N. Soda St.

Frame with clapboarding, 48'4" (five-bay front) x 48'4", two-story main section with one-story additions, gable and shed roofs, two-story one-bay portico with balcony and pedimented roof, end chimneys; center hall plan. Built c. 1870 by Buckner Abernathy; addition to rear c. 1957. 8 sheets (1966, including plans, elevations, section); 3 ext. photos (1966), 2 int. photos (1966); 4 data pages (1966). NR.

Alley House (See *Duke, W. S., House*)

Alley, D. N., Sr., House (Ward House) (TEX-117)
209 E. Broadway

Frame with clapboarding, L-shaped, five-bay front, one-and-a-half stories, gabled roof with central attic gable; on west facade, hexastyle Doric portico shelters elaborately carved entrance with sidelights and fan-shaped pediment, four floor length windows, and a corner pilaster opposite each end column; on the southeast, an L-shaped portico with seven square columns connects main section and rear wing. Built c. 1850 by D. N. Alley, Sr., as dower house for his daughter; sold in 1876 to W. B. Ward, a leading businessman. The "1881 Club," oldest chartered club in Texas, was organized here in October 1881. 4 ext. photos (1936); 1 data page (1936).

Alley-Carlson House (TEX-152)
501 E. Walker St.

Frame, 48' (five-bay front) x 44', one story, gabled roof, fluted Doric tetrastyle portico; center hall plan, dining room finished in unpainted molded cypress boards applied vertically. Built 1859; two-owner house, little altered, contains original furnishings. Typical mid-19th century house of the area.

2 ext. photos (1966), 2 int. photos (1966) ; 4 data pages (1966). NR.

Beard House (See *Birge, Noble A., House*)

Birge, Noble A., House (Beard House) (TEX-113)
212 N. Vale St. at Henderson St.

Frame with clapboarding, 43′ (five-bay front) x 55′4″ (76′5½″ with rear addition), one story, low-pitched shingled hipped roof with simple cresting, wide box cornice and bracketed eaves, two flat-roofed porticos (distyle portico at main entrance sheltering double entrance door with horizontal transom; tetrastyle portico on side sheltering two windows and door with elliptical transom) both having full entablatures, bracketed frieze and attenuated columns in form of Greek cross in section, brick chimneys and foundation piers; irregular plan with seven rooms, center hall, side hall, and rear wing. Built c. 1860 by Noble A. Birge, merchant; occupied by George R. Beard until his death in 1884. One of few buildings in or near business center of Jefferson to survive fire of 1866; kitchen extension added to east side in 1900; restored 1950's. 3 sheets (1959, including plot plan, plan, elevations) ; 3 ext. photos (1936) ; 1 data page (1936). HABSI. NR.

Camp Building (Jefferson Journal Building) (TEX-111)
112 N. Vale St.

Brick, rectangular (three-bay front), two stories with coffered brick parapet, three French doors and marquise across front, three windows above with segmental arched mouldings and consoles opening on second-story cast-iron balcony. Built c. 1850, when Jefferson was closely related to New Orleans commercially; design of building shows New Orleans precedent. Originally known as Camp Building. Occupied during Civil War by Col. A. G. Malloy, officer in Quartermasters Dept., Confederate Army, and used as recruiting office for troops. After 1864, used as bank and known as Harrison Bank Building. Now automotive supply house. 3 ext. photos (1936) ; 1 data page (1936).

Catholic Church (See Immaculate Conception [Roman] Catholic Church)

Christ Episcopal Church (TEX-143)
NW. corner of Main and Taylor Streets

Frame with brick veneer, rectangular with modern brick ell, 31'1½" (one-bay front) x 68' (four-bay side plus 8' projecting narthex), one story, gabled roof, side bays separated by brick buttresses; two-aisled nave and chancel, windows and main door have pointed-arch surrounds, hammer-beam truss ceiling in nave, Gothic Revival details. Built 1868; attributed to E. G. Benners. Original frame building sheathed with brick after storm damage in 1898; early steeple removed. 5 sheets (1966, including site plan, plan, elevations, details); 1 ext. photo (1966), 1 int. photo (1966); 4 data pages (1966).

Cockell House (See *Cutrer-Key House*)

Culberson House (Culbertson House) (TEX-114)
403 N. Walnut St.

Frame with clapboarding, five-bay front, one story, hipped roof covers main section and hexastyle portico with square columns on main facade; gable roofs cover rear addition and distyle portico on west facade. Built c. 1850 by Reverend D. B. Culberson, whose grandson, Charles A. Culberson, served as Attorney General and Governor of Texas before becoming United States Senator. 3 ext. photos (1936); 1 data page (1936).

Cutrer-Key House (Cockell House) (TEX-116)
E. side Tex. 59, 1.7 mile S. of Jefferson

Frame, L-shaped, 48'4" (five-bay front) x 40'5", rear wing (43'7" x 20') connected to main house by breezeway, one story on piers, hipped roof, tetrastyle portico with flat roof, double entrance door with straight transom and side lights, rear gallery; center hall plan, Greek Revival details. Rear wing probably built late 1840's; main house built 1869; piers beneath wing enclosed to form lower story c. 1936; some interior alterations in both sections. 10 sheets (1966, including location map, plans, elevations, sections, details); 4 ext. photos (1936, 1966), 2 int. photos (1966); 6 data pages (1966).

DeWare House, Jefferson/Jack E. Boucher, Photo 1966

DeWare House (TEX-149)
202 E. Dixon St.

Wooden frame with board and batten finish, 60' (seven-bay front) x 18', rear wing approx. 28' x 50', one story, gable roof, end chimneys, porch across front with large square pillars, "gingerbread" at eaves, and open work balustrade; modified center hall plan. Built c. 1850. 4 ext. photos (1966); 4 data pages (1966).

Duke, W. S., House (Keese House, Alley House) (TEX-119)
112 S. Friou St.

Frame with clapboarding (five-bay front), one story, gable roof with plain wide cornice and returns, fluted Doric tetra-style portico, rear ell with gable roof and shed addition, two exterior brick chimneys on west gable end of main section. Built between 1866 and 1870 for W. S. Duke and wife. 2 ext. photos (1936) ; 1 data page (1937).

Epperson, Benjamin H., House (See *House of the Seasons*)

Excelsior Hotel (TEX-112)
NW. side Austin St., between Market and Vale Sts.

Original section: frame, 71' x 34'2", two stories, hipped roof, central hall. Probably built by William Perry c. 1858-59; main doorway moved 1954. Section at southwest end (forming ell with original building): brick 29'11" x 100'6", two stories, hipped roof behind brick parapet, decorative brick cornice; first floor public rooms, second floor guest rooms. Built c. 1872. Porch across both facades has cast-iron columns and railing. Hotel restored 1961, museum installed in one room of brick section. Continuously operated as hotel since 1850's. 7 sheets (1966, including plans, elevations, sections, details) ; 5 ext. photos (1936, 1966), 5 int. photos (1936, 1966) ; 7 data pages (1966). NR.

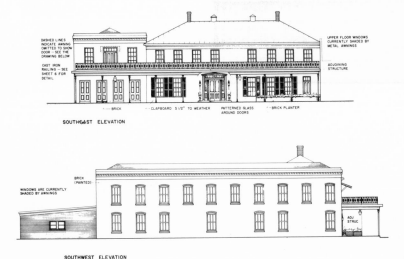

Excelsior Hotel, Jefferson/Bob J. Fong, Del. 1966

Excelsior Hotel, Registration Desk/Jack E. Boucher, Photo 1966

Freeman, Williamson M., House (TEX-33-D-3)
S. side of Tex. 49, 0.8 mile W. of Jefferson

Frame and brick, 48′1¾″ (five-bay front) x 38′1″, Louisiana raised-cottage type with one-story clapboarded frame portion above fully exposed brick basement, main entrance reached by broad flight of stairs rising one story to tetrastyle giant Doric portico, house and portico both covered by shallow hipped roof, full entablature with box cornice; center hall plan with four large chambers on each level, Greek Revival details. Built c. 1850 by Williamson M. Freeman, cotton planter and manufacturer; purchased by Texas Society, DAR in 1971 for use as museum and library. 5 sheets (1934, including plans, elevations, sections, details) ; 10 ext. photos (1934) ; 2 data pages (1934, 1971). NR.

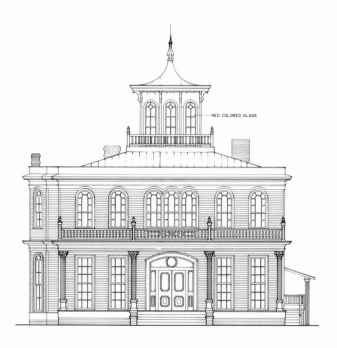

RED COLORED GLASS

House of the Seasons (Benjamin H. Epperson House), Jefferson/
Bob Fong, Del. 1966

House of the Seasons (Benjamin H. Epperson House)
(TEX-142)
409 S. Alley St.

Frame, L-shaped, 50'7" (five-bay front) x 47'6", two stories,
hipped roof, square cupola with colored glass windows representing the seasons of the year, balustraded captain's walk,
one-story balustraded porch with Corinthian columns, round-
arched windows on second floor, side bay and cupola; center
hall plan with stair in side hall, circular well open from first
floor to cupola, frescoes in drawing room and cupola dome,
built-in bookcases in study, original gas fixtures remain.
Rare example of Italianate style in northeast Texas. Built
c. 1872 by Benjamin H. Epperson, locally prominent lawyer
and railroad developer, few alterations, once-detached kitch-
en now forms rear ell. 14 sheets (1966, including plans,
elevations, sections, details) ; 5 ext. photos (1966), 7 int.
photos (1966) ; 6 data pages (1966). NR.

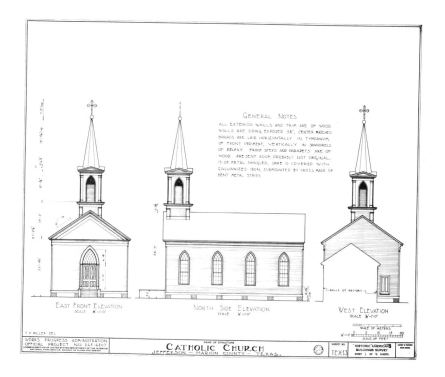

Immaculate Conception Catholic Church, Jefferson/T. P. Miller, Del. 1937

Immaculate Conception (*Roman*) *Catholic Church* (Catholic
   Church) (TEX-13)
201 N. Vale St. at corner of W. Lafayette St.

Frame, clapboarded, 31'3" (one-bay front) x 56'3" (four-
bay side), one story, gable roof, pedimented front gable
with full entablature, three-stage tower (square base, louvered belfry, and spire surmounted by metal cross) across
front gable, windows and main door have lancet-arched
mouldings and transoms; open plan with central and side
aisles, sanctuary flanked by side altars, rear balcony, walls
paneled with matched wooden boards painted white. Built
1867; Bernard Whitcorn, builder; in 1870, moved about
100 yards to present location; restored 1967. 4 sheets (1937,
including plan, elevations, sections, details); 2 ext. photos
(1936), 2 int. photos (1936); 1 data page (1936).

Jefferson Historical Society Museum (See *U. S. Courthouse and Post Office*)

Jefferson Courthouse (Old Jefferson Court House) (TEX-118)
304 W. Broadway

Brick, rectangular (three-bay front, nine-bay side), two stories, gable roof, full height tetrastyle portico on main facade has giant unfluted Doric columns, full entablature, and pediment with diamond-shaped window, other windows have segmental-arched mouldings and consoles, Greek Revival style. Built 1870-74 as Courthouse on land donated to town by Daniel N. Alley, a founder of Jefferson; Thomas Hinkle, architect. Later used as school for Negroes in Jefferson County Public School System; early photographs show tall cupola, absent in 1936; building destroyed by fire in 1942. 1 ext. photo (1936) ; 1 data page (1936).

Jefferson Journal Building (See *Camp Building*)

Kahn Saloon Building (TEX-110)
123 W. Austin St., at Vale St.

Brick, rectangular (three-bay front), two stories, arcaded first floor front with ashlar-scored stucco, flat roof with full entablature. Built 1865 for Kahn and used as saloon for many years; later used as office building. Typical of mid-19th century commercial architecture in Jefferson. 2 ext. photos (1936) ; 1 data page (1937).

Keese House (See *Duke, W. S., House*)

Murphy-Dannelly House (TEX-148)
410 Delta St., SW. corner of Delta and Main Sts.

Frame, main block 51'7" (five-bay front) x 35'8", two stories, gabled roof, two story portico at main entrance; center hall plan. Built between 1850 and 1860; rear ell added c. 1864; extensive renovation in 1951 included addition of west wing and alteration of portico. 8 sheets (1966, including plans, elevations, section) ; 1 ext. photo (1966), 1 int. photo (1966) ; 5 data pages (1966).

Old Jefferson Court House (See *Jefferson Courthouse*)

Planters Bank Building and Warehouse (TEX-144)
224 E. Austin St.

Bank section: brick, 35'9" (four-bay front) x 45'9", two stories, parallel gable roofs behind a brick parapet, four French doors across front with cast-iron balcony above; open first floor with teller's enclosure, 3 rooms on second floor. Warehouse (extension behind bank): brick, 89'2" long, now one story with flat roof, open plan. Built c. 1852 by John Speake; upper story of warehouse removed after fire. One of few extant business structures of this type from era when Jefferson was the largest inland port in the Southwest. 4 sheets (1966, including plans, elevations, section), 2 ext. photos (1966); 5 data pages (1966). NR.

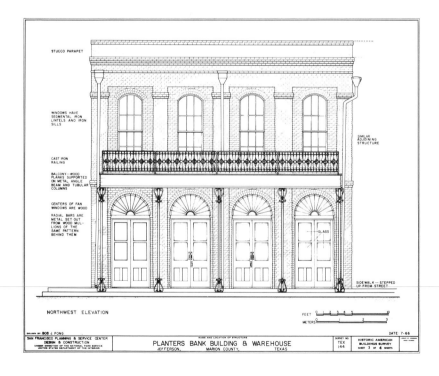

Planters Bank Building and Warehouse, Jefferson/Bob J. Fong, Del. 1966

Presbyterian Church (TEX-150)
600 E. Jefferson St.

Brick, 46' (three-bay front) x 75' (five-bays), one story on raised basement, gabled roof, two-aisle plan with recessed chancel; central projecting entrance tower, octagonal spire, corbeled cornice and decorative details of brick; Gothic Revival details. Built 1873. 3 ext. photos (1966), 2 int. photos (1966); 5 data pages (1966).

Presbyterian Manse (General Rogers House) (TEX-14)
221 Delta St. at Alley St.

Frame with clapboarding, 50'5" (five-bay front) x 40'3½", one story, low U-shaped hipped roof, tetrastyle portico at main entrance with full entablature, fluted columns and hipped roof, double entrance door with straight transom and side lights, tetrastyle portico on side, hexastyle portico across rear; center hall plan, Greek Revival details. Built 1853; purchased by General James Harrison Rogers in 1856. Said to be oldest house still standing in Jefferson. 6 sheets (1936, 1938, including site plan, plans, elevations, sections, details); 4 ext. photos (1936), 2 int. photos (1936); 1 data page (1936), HABSI. NR.

Rogers, General, House (See *Presbyterian Manse*)

St. Mary's (Roman) Catholic School and Sinai Hebrew Synagogue (TEX-141)
209 N. Henderson St.

Two frame buildings joined by a covered passageway. School building: 48'4" (four-bay front) x 20'4", two stories raised on piers, hipped roof, two-story tetrastyle portico, wide wooden cornice; center hall plan, Greek Revival details. Synagogue: 37'3" x 33'1", one tall story, gable roof; one room plan with balcony, original ark remains. School built before 1869; property deeded to Hebrew Congregation 1874; synagogue built 1876, W. F. J. Graham, builder; school has rear addition, synagogue has minor interior alterations. Secularized 1954: school unused; synagogue used as theatre. 10 sheets (1966, including site plans, plans, elevations, sections, details) ; 4 ext. photos (1966), 2 int. photos (1966) ; 5 data pages (1966). NR.

Sedberry House (TEX-151)
211 N. Market St.

Frame and brick, 45′ (five-bay front), rear ell extends 36′, raised cottage type with story-and-a-half frame portion above fully exposed brick basement, gabled roof with small cross-gable, tetrastyle portico with fluted wooden Doric columns above brick piers, ornamental cast-iron stairs curve up to each end of portico, bracketed cornice; center hall plan. Built c. 1870. 4 ext. photos (1966), 2 int. photos (1966) ; 4 data pages (1966). NR.

Spellings House (TEX-115)
107 E. Clarksville St.

Frame with clapboarding, five-bay front, one story, hipped roof on main section, shed and gable roofs on additions, cornice with wide frieze, tetrastyle portico with square columns sheltering double entrance door with straight transom and side lights, brick end chimneys and foundation piers. Built c. 1850 by Solomon A. Spellings, prominent member of the community. 3 ext. photos (1936) ; 1 data page (1936).

U. S. Courthouse and Post Office (now *Jefferson Historical Society Museum*) (TEX-140)
224 W. Austin St.

Museum. Brick, L-shaped, 52′7″ (three-bay front) x 70′7″, two-and-a-half stories on raised basement, hipped roof on front section, high gable roof on rear courtroom section, four-stage hip-roofed entrance tower, first floor used for post office, second floor for courts, Romanesque Revival style. Built 1888-90; Will A. Freret, Supervising Architect of the Treasury. Converted to a museum, 1965. 12 sheets (1966, including plans, elevations, section, details) ; 4 ext. photos (1966), 1 int. photo (1966), photocopy of lithograph of plans and perspective (1887), copy of old photo (1889) ; 9 data pages (1966). NR.

U. S. Courthouse and Post Office, Jefferson/Jack E. Boucher, Photo 1966

Ward House (See *Alley, D. N., Sr., House*)

Wibler-Woods House (TEX-153)
502 E. Walker St.

Frame, 48' (five-bay front) x 36', one story, parallel gable roofs with connecting roof; decorative roof cresting, finials, and bargeboards; classical tetrastyle portico shelters double entrance door with side lights and transom; modified center hall plan, tall narrow windows with interior louvered shutters. Built c. 1865; small rear addition c. 1900. 3 ext. photos (1966), 2 int. photos (1966); 5 data pages (1966). NR.

Wright-Lester House (TEX-145)
301 S. Friou St.

Frame, main block 52'6" (five-bay front) x 36'5", two stories, gable roof, center hall plan. Originally a story-and-a-half structure built c. 1859; raised to two stories after mid-20th-century fire destroyed original roof; one-story additions across rear and two-story front portico added 1941. 3 sheets (1966, including plot plan, plan, construction details) ; 2 ext. photos (1966), 2 int. photos (1966) ; 4 data pages (1966).

KARNACK VICINITY   Harrison County (102)

Andrews-Taylor House (TEX-147)
3 mi. SW. of Karnack on Tex. 43, E. of intersection with Farm Rd. 2862

Brick, L-shaped, 56'3" (five-bay front) x 40'8" (including ell), two stories, hipped roofs, two-story pedimented entrance portico, two-story rear porch shelters cantilevered balcony which gives access to second floor rooms, exterior stairway; center hall plan. Built 1843; George W. Taloo, builder; 20th-century additions. Childhood home of Mrs. Lyndon Johnson. 11 sheets (1966, including plans, elevations, details) ; 7 ext. photos (1966), 1 int. photo (1966) ; 6 data pages (1966).

KIMBALL   Bosque County (18)

Kimball Academy (TEX-139)
Tex. 174, west bank of Brazos River

Limestone, 35' x 60', one story roofless and ruinous. The remains of a private academy built in 1873. 6 ext. photos (1961) ; 5 data pages (1962).

KINGSBURY VICINITY   Guadalupe County (94)

McCulloch, Ben, House (TEX-353)

Adobe and plaster, one story, gabled roof, with clapboarded gable end; cabin type. Built 1850's by T. H. Holloman, sold

Andrews-Taylor House, Karnack Vicinity/Jack E. Boucher, Photo 1966

to McCulloch, a cannoneer in the Battle of San Jacinto. Ruinous. 2 ext. photos (1936) ; 1 data page (1936).

LA GRANGE   Fayette County (75)

Etario Club (See *Stiehl, Judge J. C., House*)

Frede, Francis, House (Kaulbach House) (TEX-3120) Gone. Formerly on or near LaFayette Street.

Wooden frame with clapboarding, one story, low-pitched gabled roof peaks sharply near ridge, creating unusual pediment above nine-column entrance porch. Built c. 1845 as a wedding gift from Francis Frede to his bride, Louise Eilers. 2 ext. photos (1936) ; 1 data page (1936).

Kaulbach House (See *Frede, Francis, House*)

Kirsch, Anton, House (TEX-3122)
Gone.

Stone and stucco, four-bay front, one-and-a-half stories, gabled pedimented entrance porch, chimney in each gable end. Built c. 1870. 3 ext. photos (1936) ; 1 data page (1936).

Judge J. C. Stiehl House (Etario Club), La Grange/
Harry Starnes, Photo 1936

Stiehl, Judge J. C., House (Etario Club) (TEX-3121)
Fannin at Franklin Street

Half-timber with brick infilling, three-bay front, one story, gabled roof; shallow hipped roof entrance porch. The hewn cedar timbers with wooden pin connections are typical of German "fachwerk" in central Texas. Built c. 1852 by Judge J. C. Stiehl, this small house was owned by a literary study club in the 1930's and is now used as a library. 4 ext. photos (1936); 1 data page (1937).

LANGTRY   Val Verde County (233)

Bean, Judge Roy, Saloon and Justice Court (Jersey Lilly Saloon) (TEX-3101)

Museum. Wooden frame with clapboarding, hipped roof, one story, gabled wing. Built 1883, it served as a combination saloon, billiard hall, and courtroom where Justice of the Peace Roy Bean earned his reputation as "the Law West of the Pecos" in the 1880's and 1890's. Restored in 1939 and maintained by the Texas Highway Department. 2 ext. photos (1900), 1 ext. photo (1936); 1 data page (1936).

LEON SPRINGS   Bexar County (15)

Aue Stagecoach Inn Complex (TEX-3220)
N. of San Antonio on Old Fredericksburg Road, W. of Interstate Hwy. 10 and E. of old Boerne-San Antonio Stage Road, now an access road to I-10.

Located on the San Antonio-Boerne Stage Road, the Aue Stagecoach Inn was established c. 1855. At that time Max Aue, one of a number of German citizens immigrating to Texas in the 1846-56 decade, procured the property and erected a one-and-a-half story dwelling house in the characteristic Texas German Style. It may have been at this time that Aue also built the log house for use as a stagehouse. In 1878, Aue erected a new two-story stagehouse. This complex, largely unchanged today, shows the evolution of a Texas

142

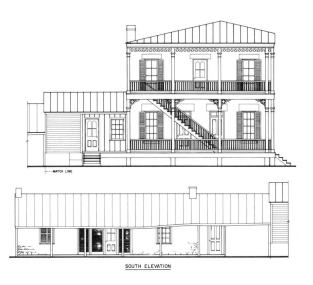

SOUTH ELEVATION

Aue Stagecoach Inn, Leon Springs/Larry Hermsen, Del. 1968

EAST ELEVATION   NORTH ELEVATION

WEST ELEVATION   SOUTH ELEVATION

Aue Stagecoach Inn/Larry Hermsen, Del. 1968

143

frontier stage stop complex and its development over three decades. 8 sheets (1968*, including site plan, plans, sections, elevations, details of the three buildings in the complex).

Photographs and data are separate for each structure:

Aue, Max, House

Limestone rubble, one-and-a-half stories, with cellar, 22' x 42', gabled, porch across front is a continuation of the roof. Typical of houses built by European immigrants to central Texas c. 1853. 3 ext. photos (1968*) ; 7 data pages (1967*). HABSI.

Aue, Max, Log House

Log, chinked and plastered, with stone additions, one story, 57' x 28', gabled, dog-trot plan, porch along south. Probably built as a stage house on the San Antonio-Boerne stage run c. 1855. 2 ext. photos (1968*) ; 3 data pages (1967*). HABSI.

Aue, Max, 1878 House

Limestone rubble, partially stuccoed, two stories, 52' x 51', hipped roof, two-story gallery on south front. Built in 1878 as a dwelling with transient rooms upstairs. Linked to the Aue log house at the west. Builder: B. Grossenbacher. 1 ext. photo (1968*) ; 6 data pages (1967*). HABSI.

LEVELLAND VICINITY   Hockley County (110)

> *Slaughter Two-story Dugout* (See LUBBOCK, Lubbock County)

LOCKHART AND VICINITY   Caldwell County (28)

> *Blackwell, James, House* (TEX-391)
> Gone.

Wooden frame, five-bay front, two stories, low-pitched gabled roof extending over a two-story porch across entire front; chimney at each gable end. Built 1857 by Charles

Crenshaw for James Blackwell, an early settler. 5 ext. photos (1936) ; 1 data page (1937).

Lane, Dr. Pleasant, House (TEX-392)
Gone.

Half-timber and wooden frame, four-bay front, two stories, gabled roof, two-story gallery across front, chimney at each main gable end. Irregular plan. Built 1852 by Capt. C. M. Lane. Dr. Pleasant Lane, one of the first physicians in the area, was from Tennessee. The second floor became a hospital during the Civil War. 5 ext. photos (1936) ; 1 data page (1937).

LUBBOCK   Lubbock County (152)

The Ranch Headquarters
E. of The Museum of Texas Tech University, near intersection of 4th and Indiana Sts.

The following entries are for early Texas ranch buildings and related structures which have been moved from various parts of the state and reassembled here where they are presented together as an outdoor museum of ranching history.

Bairfield School (TEX-3243)
Originally on Farm Road 262, 1 mile SW. of Clarendon, Donley County

Box and strip construction (modified board and batten) with later horizontal siding, rock fittings, 14′ x 16′, one story, gabled roof. One room. Cedar posts attached to building at sides and corners and driven into ground to keep it from blowing away. Built late 1880's, moved to present location 1972. 4 sheets (1973, including site plans, plan, elevations, section, details).

Harrell House (TEX-3235)
Originally approx. 10 miles N. of Snyder, Scurry County

Stone and box and strip, 50′ x 68′, one story, gable roof, front and side porches, irregular plan. Stone portion built c. 1883, first box and strip addition before

1899, second between 1899-1913. Semi-restored at original location 1961-63. Moved to present location 1972. 5 sheets (1972, including site plan, plan, elevations, details).

Hedwigs Hill Cabin (TEX-3233)
Originally 9 miles SE. of Mason, Mason County, via U.S. 87

Log with stone additions, stuccoed, 42′ x 23′10″, one-and-a-half stories, gable roof with chimneys at each gabled end. Typical double log cabin connected by covered breezeway, or "dog run," from which a straight run of stairs leads to the attic. Log portion built mid-1850's. Moved to present location 1971. 6 sheets (1971, including site plan, plans, elevations, sections, details).

"J A" Milk and Meat Cooler (TEX-3236)
Originally approx. 24 miles SE. of Claude, Armstrong County, via Tex. 207 and Farm Road 2272

Stone, board, and latticework, 31′ x 14′, one story, low gable roof of split poles covered with mud. Two rooms, one for meat, one for milk. An ingenious structure with water troughs for cooling and latticework for evaporation, keeping temperatures low enough to prevent spoilage. Perhaps as early as 1878. Moved to present location 1970. 3 sheets (1973, including site plans, plan, elevations).

Jowell Ranch House (TEX-3237)
Originally near S. shore of Possum Kingdom Lake, approx. 13 miles NW. of Palo Pinto, Palo Pinto County

Limestone, coursed rubble with quoins, 17′ x 12′, two stories, ruinous. Built mid-1870's, abandoned 1881, moved to present location 1973. 3 sheets (1972, including site plan, plans, elevations, sections).

"Long S" Box and Strip House (TEX-3241)
Originally in NW. corner of Martin County, SW. of Patricia

Box and strip construction, 24' (two-bay front) x 20', one story, gable roof, front porch, rear lean-to. Four room plan. Built c. 1900, moved to present location 1973. 2 sheets (1973, including site plans, plan, elevations).

Masterson Rock Bunkhouse (TEX-3231)
Originally approx. 15 miles W. of Truscott, King County

Limestone, coursed, 17' x 15', one story, gable roof, chimney at E. end, front porch with shed roof. Built c. 1879. Moved to present location 1971. 3 sheets (1971, including site plan, plan, elevations, section, detail).

Matador Guest House and Office (TEX-3262)
Originally 1 mile S. of Matador, Motley County, W. side of Tex. 70

Wooden frame with clapboarding, 37' x 18', one story, gable roof, porch which extends across front and E. side has ornamental posts and brackets. Built c. 1900. Moved to present location 1972. 4 sheets (1972, including site plans, plan, elevations, details).

Matador Half-Dugout (TEX-3232)
Originally approx. 16 miles NE. of Dickens, Dickens County

Log with stone foundation, 19' x 15', one story, gable roof, sandstone chimney. Although not built until c. 1890, this structure is representative of much earlier building types. Moved to present location 1971. 2 sheets (1971, including site plan, plan, elevations, section).

Slaughter Two-story Dugout (TEX-3228)
Originally 13 miles NW. of Levelland, Hockley County

Box and strip, 14' x 18', two stories, gable roof, later sheltered entryway, 8' x 7', with steps down to lower dugout room, steps up to upper level, an early example of a "split-foyer." Built c. 1890, second level added before 1912. Moved to present location 1971. 3 sheets (1971, including site plan, plans, elevations, section).

Spur-Swenson Granary (TEX-3230)
Originally 8 miles W. of Dickens, Dickens County

Box and strip on random rubble limestone foundation, 96' x 15'9", one and two stories, incorporating stable, manger and feed room on lower level, granary on second, from which feed flows through chutes to grain box below. Built c. 1895. Moved to present location 1971. 6 sheets (1971, including site plan, plans, elevations, sections, details).

"U Lazy S" Carriage, Saddle and Harness House (TEX-3242)
Originally approx. 10 miles S. of Post, Garza County, W. side of Farm Road 669

Box and strip, 50' x 14', two stories, shed roof; partitioned into spaces for carriages, tack room, and feed storage. Built after 1901. Moved to present location 1970. 2 sheets (1972, including site plans, plans, elevations).

Bairfield School, Lubbock/Elizabeth Sasser, Del. 1973

148

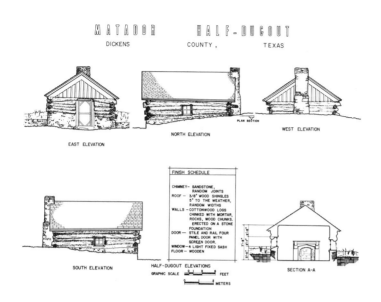

MATADOR HALF-DUGOUT
DICKENS   COUNTY,   TEXAS

EAST ELEVATION

NORTH ELEVATION

PLAN SECTION

WEST ELEVATION

SOUTH ELEVATION

HALF-DUGOUT ELEVATIONS
GRAPHIC SCALE   FEET   METERS

SECTION A-A

FINISH SCHEDULE

CHIMNEY— SANDSTONE, RANDOM JOINTS
ROOF — 3/8" WOOD SHINGLES, 5" TO THE WEATHER, RANDOM WIDTHS
WALLS —COTTONWOOD LOGS CHINKED WITH MORTAR, ROCKS, WOOD CHUNKS. ERECTED ON A STONE FOUNDATION
DOOR — STILE AND RAIL FOUR PANEL DOOR WITH SCREEN DOOR.
WINDOW—4 LIGHT FIXED SASH
FLOOR — WOODEN

Matador Half-Dugout, Lubbock/Ray G. Pinkerton, Del. 1971

NORTH ELEVATION

EAST ELEVATION

SOUTH ELEVATION

WEST ELEVATION

FEET   METERS   SCALE 3/8"=1'-0"

Masterson Rock Bunkhouse, Lubbock/Walter R. Kilroy, Del. 1971

149

LUFKIN VICINITY

Angelina County (3)

Gann, John, House (TEX-285)
10 miles SW. of Lufkin via Tex. 94

Log, five-bay front, one story, gable roof, enclosed dog-trot breezeway with full-length porch, additions at rear. Built 1836-40, it has been moved once. 2 ext. photos (1936); 1 data page (1937).

MARSHALL AND VICINITY

Harrison County (102)

Alexander House (TEX-124)
Gone

Wooden frame with clapboarding and board and batten, one story with raised basement, hip roof with square cupola, ground floor entrance at side, first floor entrance at front, reached by flight of steps to square-columned veranda around three sides. Built c. 1860. 3 ext. photos (1936); 1 data page (1936).

Carter House (TEX-121)
Gone

Wooden frame, five-bay front, one story, gable roof, chimney at each end, porches around front and one side. Irregular plan. Floor-length windows. Built 1860. 3 ext. photos (1936), 1 data page (1936).

First Methodist Church South (First United Methodist Church) (TEX-122)
300 E. Houston St.

Brick, stuccoed, gable roof, five-bay nave with plain stuccoed cornice and pilasters, square-columned tetrastyle front portico. Built c. 1850. Although alterations and additions have been made on numerous occasions, the building maintains a unified design. 2 ext. photos (1936); 1 data page (1936).

J. B. Henderson House, Marshall Vicinity/Harry Starnes, Photo 1936

Henderson, J. B., House (TEX-120)
4.8 miles N. of Marshall on U.S. 59

Random ashlar first floor, wooden frame with clapboarding above, two stories, gable roof, six-column giant portico shelters continuous second-floor balcony, with ornamental railing. Chimney at each gable end is of ashlar through beginning of second floor, brick above. Built 1860 by J. B. Henderson of North Carolina, and for several years used as a stagecoach stop on the route from Shreveport, Louisiana, to Jefferson, Texas. 3 ext. photos (1936); 1 data page (1936).

Holcombe, B. L., House (See *"Wyalucing"*)

Munce House (TEX-123)
Gone

Brick, frame and clapboarding, one story, gable roof, six-column porch across front. L-plan. Built c. 1860 by Philip Hendricks. 2 ext. photos (1936) ; 1 data page (1936).

Whetstone House (TEX-125)

Wooden frame, three-bay front, two stories, gable roof, giant pedimented portico with four square columns shelters spindled second-floor balcony above front entrance. Built 1865. 3 ext. photos (1936) ; 1 data page (1936).

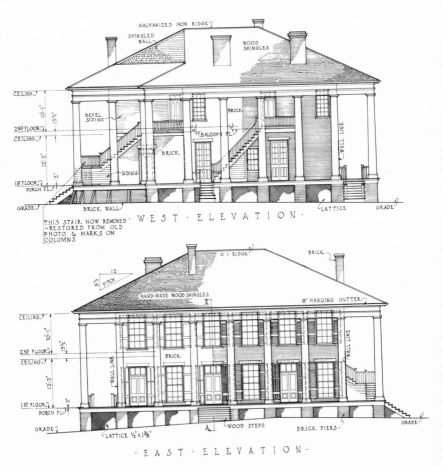

"Wyalucing" (B. L. Holcombe House), Marshall/
C. Frank Dunham Jr., Del. 1934

"Wyalucing" (B. L. Holcombe House) (TEX-33-D-4)
Gone. Formerly Bishop and West Rush Sts.

Brick, 58'11" (six-bay front) x 77'10", two stories, hip roof, two-story colonnade on high podium, tapered rectangular columns. Built 1850 by Beverly Lafayette Holcombe. Used as classroom and music building by Bishop College from 1880-1961, razed 1962. "Wyalucing," an Indian name meaning "Home of the Friendless," was an estate of about 100 acres devoted exclusively to household uses, and separate from the Holcombe plantation. Holcombe's daughter, Lucy, a renowned beauty whose portrait adorned Confederate $100 bills, was the wife of the governor of South Carolina, Francis W. Pickens. 5 sheets (1934, including site plan, plans, elevations, sections, details) ; 8 ext. photos (1934), 1 int. photo (1934) ; 2 data pages (1936).

MASON VICINITY   Mason County (160)

Hedwigs Hill Cabin (See LUBBOCK, Lubbock County)

MATADOR VICINITY   Motley County (173)

Matador Guest House and Office (See LUBBOCK, Lubbock County)

MILAM VICINITY   Sabine County (202)

Gaines-McGowan House (TEX-267)
Dismantled for preservation

Log, one story, gable roof, dog-trot plan, with roof extending over rear lean-to and recessed six-post front entrance porch. Built 1820 at the strategic crossing of the Sabine River and El Camino Real. The crossing was known as Gaines Ferry, later as Pendleton's Ferry. Before the site was submerged by the Toledo Bend Reservoir, the house was disassembled for preservation, but it has not been reconstructed. 1 ext. photo (1936) ; 1 data page (1936).

Davidson, Quincy, House (TEX-248)
Gone

Wooden frame, two stories, gable roof, narrow pedimented two-story entrance porch. Built 1861 by pioneer cattleman of lumber imported from Florida. 1 ext. photo (1936); 1 data page (1936).

De Leon, Patricio, Ranch House (TEX-278)
Gone

Log, weatherboarded, one story, gable roof, stone fireplace chimney. Built 1839. 1 ext. photo (1936); 1 data page (1936).

James Rives House, Mission Valley/Harry Starnes, Photo 1936

Rives, James, House (TEX-246)
Gone

Wooden frame, two stories, very shallow gable roof reaching over two-story front porch and rear extension; chimney at each gable end. Built 1875. 1 ext. photo (1936); 1 data page (1936).

NACOGDOCHES AND VICINITY
Nacogdoches County (174)

Bean, Peter Ellis, House (TEX-236)
E. of Nacogdoches on Melrose Road

Log with weatherboard and clapboarding, one story, gable roof with chimney at each gable end; rectangular plan with roof extended over raised six-post porch. Built c. 1829. Bean, a native of Tennessee, became an officer in the Mexican army, serving as commandant at Nacogdoches until the Texas Revolution, when he was interned. After Texas became independent, he moved to Mexico. The house has been altered beyond recognition. 1 ext. photo (1936); 1 data page (1936).

Hoya Library (See *Sterne, Adolphus, House*)

Nacogdoches University (TEX-235)
High School Grounds - Washington Square

Brick, three-bay front, two stories, Greek Revival temple form with tetrastyle Doric portico and louvered octagonal cupola. Built 1858-59. When the university closed in 1904 the building was used by the public schools of Nacogdoches. Restored. 1 ext. photo (1936); 1 data page (1936). NR.

Sacred Heart Church (See CENTER—*Church of the Divine Infant*)

Sterne, Adolphus, House (Hoya Library) (TEX-234)
211 LaNana St.

Library-Museum. Wooden frame, one story, gable roof, chimney at each gable end, hip roof, front and side porches. Built 1830, and until 1852 the home of German-born Adolphus

Nacogdoches University, Nacogdoches/Harry Starnes, Photo 1936

Sterne, who came from Cologne via New Orleans. "Alcalde," or mayor, of Nacogdoches, Sterne was a friend of Sam Houston and supplier of money and men for the Texas Revolution. 2 ext. photos (1936), 1 int. photo (1936); 2 data pages (1936).

Ybarbo Ranch House (TEX-268)
On grounds of Stephen F. Austin College

Log, one story, gable roof, adobe chimney at one end, lean-to porch across front. The original site on Lobanella Creek near Geneva was settled by Antonio Gil y Barbo c. 1773; the attribution of this house to him is highly conjectural. 2 ext. photos (1936); 2 data pages (1936).

Bechtol House (Navasota Beauty Shop) (TEX-216)
Gone

Wooden frame, one story, front portion flat-roofed, porch had wide entablature and six square columns. 1 ext. photo (1936).

Collins-Camp House (Foster House) (Former Alfred Felder Home) (TEX-215)
Gone

Wooden frame with clapboarding, two stories, gable roof with two-story gabled entrance porch. Built 1860's by Alfred Felder. 3 ext. photos (1936).

Collins-Camp House, Navasota Vicinity/Harry Starnes, Photo 1936

Foster House (See *Collins-Camp House*)

Freeman, Ira M., House (TEX-271)
Gone

Wooden frame, two stories, gable roof. Already near collapse in 1936. The house was built about 1858 for Freeman, a merchant who came to Texas from Kentucky in 1845. 1 ext. photo (1936) ; 1 data page (1936).

Gibbs-Foster House (TEX-214)
2 miles NE. on Tex. 90

Wooden frame, five-bay front, two-and-a-half stories, gable roof with gabled dormers and chimneys at each gable end; rectangular plan. Porch across front with six square columns, recessed porch at rear. Center-hall plan. Built about 1859 by Malcolm Camp for his son-in-law, Jeff Gibbs, Republican sheriff of Grimes County during Reconstruction era. 2 ext. photos (1936) ; 1 data page (1936).

Navasota Beauty Shop (See *Bechtol House*)

NEW BRAUNFELS Comal County (46)

Ervendberg Orphanage ("Waisenhaus") (West Texas Orphan Asylum) (TEX-3145)
W. bank of Guadalupe River off Ervendberg Avenue

Half-timber ("fachwerk"), with adobe brick infilling and weatherboard covering, 39′ (five-bay front) x 55′, one story, U-plan, opening toward the rear, with gable roofs extending over porch across front. The West Texas Orphan Asylum was incorporated in 1848 to support and educate the orphaned children of immigrants and settlers who were victims of cholera. The Rev. Louis Ervendberg, one of the incorporators, undertook the care of 19 children in addition to his own family in this house, which was built for that purpose in 1850 by Johann Heinrich Meine. This first orphanage in Texas operated only until 1855. 2 ext. photos (1961), 1 int. photo (1961) ; 6 data pages (1963) ; HABSI.

Forke, J. L., House (TEX-373)
Gone. Formerly at rear of 593 Seguin St.

Half-timber with brick and adobe infilling and weatherboarding, three-bay front, one story, gable roof, three-room rectangle with porch along one side. Built in the 1850's and sold to J. L. Forke, Sr. in 1856. 3 ext. photos (1936) ; 1 data page (1936).

Hinman, Heinrich, House (TEX-3253)
Castell Avenue between San Antonio and Coll Sts.

Limestone ashlar, 40'5" (five-bay front) x 38'8" with later rear and side additions, two stories, low gable roof, two-tiered front porch. Built 1868. Interior plan, finish, and trim much altered. 7 sheets (1972, including site plan, plans, elevations, section, details) ; 5 ext. photos (1972), 1 int. photo (1972) ; 6 data pages (1972).

SOUTHWEST ELEVATION – FRONT

Heinrich Hinman House, New Braunfels/Roy Pledger, Del. 1972

159

Heinrich Hinman House/Roy Pledger, Photo 1972

Homann, Friederich, Saddlery and Residence (New Braunfels Coffee Company) (TEX-33-A-11)
Gone. Formerly 136 Seguin St.

Brick and stucco, 46′ (five-bay front) x 36′3″, two stories,
low-pitched gable roof, overhanging bracketed front cornice.
Built for Friederich Homann c. 1850, the lower floor was used
as a saddlery, the upper floor as a home for the Homann
family. One of the first pretentious buildings in New Braunfels, it had a parlor nearly 25′ square for entertaining. 3
sheets (1934, including plans, elevations, sections, details);
12 ext. photos, some emphasizing iron footscrapers (1934),
1 int. photo (1934); 2 data pages (1936). HABSI.

Klein-Naegelin House (Naegelin House) (TEX-33-A-10)
511 S. Seguin Ave.

Half-timber frame ("fachwerk") with stone nogging, plastered, 28'2" x 20'8", one story, gable roof with lesser pitch over front porch and rear kitchen. Original two-room central portion built c. 1846 for Stephan Klein. 4 sheets (1934, including plans, elevations, sections, details); 7 ext. photos (1934), 1 ext. photo (1972); 4 data pages (1972). NR.

Landa Rock Mill (TEX-3251)
Landa Street near entrance to Landa Park

Limestone ashlar, 30' (three-bay front) x 74', three stories, low gable roof with parapet end walls; open plan. Built 1875 by Joseph Landa, later additions of frame and sheetmetal obscure end walls. 1 ext. photo (1972), 1 int. photo (1972); 5 data pages (1972).

Lindheimer, Ferdinand, House (TEX-374)
491 S. Comal Ave.

House museum. Half-timber frame ("fachwerk") with brick nogging, plastered, 28'6" x 24' with later rear lean-to having exposed "fachwerk" and stone nogging, one story, gable roof, double house plan. Original portion built c. 1852, when Lindheimer was turning from a career as a noted botanist on the frontier to become a journalist. His "Neu Braunfelser Zeitung" was published in this house for 20 years. Later clapboard siding was removed in the 1960's restoration by the New Braunfels Conservation Society. 5 sheets (1972, including site plan, plans, elevations, sections); 2 ext. photos (1936), 4 ext. photos (1972), 4 int. photos (1972); 6 data pages (1972). NR.

Naegelin House (See *Klein-Naegelin House*)

New Braunfels Coffee Company (See *Homann, Friederich, Saddlery and Residence*)

Schmidt, Phillip, House (TEX-372)
354 Bridge St.

Adobe and wood, two-bay front, one story, steep gable roof with recessed porch across front. Enclosed center hall. Built by Phillip Kleinhan before 1855, a typical early Texas German house. 2 ext. photos (1936); 1 data page (1937).

"Waisenhaus" (See *Ervendberg Orphanage*)

West Texas Orphan Asylum (See *Ervendberg Orphanage*)

NEWCASTLE VICINITY   Young County (252)

Fort Belknap (TEX-33-D-7)
3 miles S. on Tex. 251

County Park. Stone, one-story structures made up this fort, established by the U. S. Army in 1851 as an outpost against Indians and abandoned in 1859 except for a brief reactivation in 1867. A team from HABS measured the site in 1934, marking the locations of ruined buildings and making drawings of a 20' x 71' forage building and a 16' x 22' magazine. Both buildings were sufficiently intact to be restored as part of a 1936 reconstruction project, but other buildings and roads were rebuilt with no apparent reference to original locations. 3 sheets (1936, including site plan, plans, elevations, section) ; 12 ext. photos (1934, 6 of each building) ; 1 data page (1934). NR.

PALESTINE   Anderson County (1)

Dorsett House (TEX-127)
Gone

Wooden frame with clapboarding, one story, gable roof with lean-to porch across entire front, roof extending over rear enclosure. Chimneys at each gable end and at one side of rear enclosure. Built c. 1860. Bought by Dorsetts 1870. 2 ext. photos (1936) ; 1 data page (1936).

Egan House (See *Red Brick Schoolhouse*)

Gathright House (See *Pessony, George, House*)

Mallard-Alexander-McNaughton House (TEX-128)
407 E. Kolstad St.

Wooden frame, five-bay front, one story, gable roof, gabled entrance porch with four pillars. Built for Judge John B. Mallard in 1848. His widow, who retained the house, married

Judge William Alexander, giving the house its second name, and it was sold to the McNaughtons in 1870. 3 ext. photos (1936) ; 1 data page (1936).

McNaughton House (See *Mallard-Alexander-McNaughton House*)

Pessony, George, House (Gathright House) (TEX-126) Gone

Wooden frame with clapboarding, one story, gable roof, pedimented entrance porch, massive classic frieze and cornice. L-plan. Built by Gathright in 1854, sold after the Civil War. 3 ext. photos (1936) ; 1 data page (1936).

George Pessony House, Palestine/Harry Starnes, Photo 1936

Red Brick Schoolhouse, Palestine/Harry Starnes, Photo 1936

Red Brick Schoolhouse (Egan House) (TEX-129)
Gone

Brick, five-bay front, one-and-a-half stories, gable roof with two gabled dormers, chimney at each gable end, pedimented, distyle, pillared porch. Built in 1852 as the girls' school of the Masonic Institute. 3 ext. photos (1936); 1 data page (1936).

Schwirter House (TEX-130)
Gone

Wooden frame with clapboarding, one story, gable roof with off-center, pedimented entrance porch over double front doors, a lean-to at rear. Built c. 1848. 3 ext. photos (1936); 1 data page (1937).

PALO PINTO VICINITY

Palo Pinto County (182)

Jowell Ranch House (See LUBBOCK, Lubbock County)

PANNA MARIA VICINITY

Karnes County (128)

Moczygamba Houses (TEX-312)
Off Farm Road 81, 1 mile W. of Tex. 123

Limestone ashlar and stucco, one story, gable roof extends over recessed four-post porch on south front; door to attic room in gable end accessible only from exterior by ladder. Father Leopold Moczygamba led the colony which settled at Panna Maria in 1854, making it the oldest Polish Catholic community in the United States. These three small Moczygamba houses, each with stone cistern fed by wooden eaves troughs, were built c. 1857, about ¼-mile apart. Now in ruinous condition, or used for hay storage, they no longer exhibit the exterior colors noted in 1936 data. 4 ext. photos (1936); 1 data page (1936).

Urbanczyk House (TEX-311)
Off Farm Road 81, 0.5 mile W. of Tex. 123

Stone, plastered, with brick rear wing addition, four-bay front, one story, gable roof extending over three-post porch on front, gabled-end attic door reachable by ladder from outside only. Built in 1865 by Joe Kyresh. 3 ext. photos (1936); 1 data page (1936).

Whetstone Ranch House (TEX-388)
Off Farm Road 81, 2 miles W. of Tex. 123

Stone rubble, stuccoed, one story with raised basement, gable roof with chimneys at each end, six-post porch, corrugated iron roof. Built c. 1850. 5 ext. photos (1936); 1 data page (1936).

PATRICIA VICINITY

Dawson County (58)

"Long S" Box and Strip House (See LUBBOCK, Lubbock County)

PAWELEKVILLE

Pawelek, Machie, House (TEX-314)
Tex. 123 at Farm Road 887

Stone and stucco, 25' x 36', one-and-a-half stories, gable roof, porch across front, exterior stair to second floor. Built in 1865, destroyed in recent rebuilding. 3 sheets (1934, including site plan, plans, elevations, section, details) ; 4 ext. photos (1934), 3 int. photos (1936) ; 1 data page (1937).

PLANTERSVILLE VICINITY

Baker, Captain Isaac, House (See *Cedar Hall*)

Cedar Hall (Captain Isaac Baker House) (TEX-225)
1½ miles NE. of Plantersville

Wooden frame, five-bay front, two stories, hip roof with two-story pedimented entrance portico. Classic Revival. Gabled addition at rear with one-story porch. Built 1854-60 by a wealthy Alabama planter. 2 ext. photos (1936) ; 1 data page (1936).

Easley, A. B., House (TEX-27)
Gone

Wooden frame, five-bay front, two stories, gable roof, T-plan. Built by A. B. Easley, planter and cattleman from Alabama, 1855-60. 2 ext. photos (1936) ; 1 data page (1936).

Markey's Seminary Dormitory (TEX-277)
W. edge of Plantersville

Wooden frame, one story, three connected gabled units slightly offset and with continuous porch along north side. The only remaining portion of a school founded in 1857 by James Markey, from Ireland, and closed in 1875. 2 ext. photos (1936) ; 1 data page (1936).

Walton, Major Peter, House (TEX-226)
Gone

Wooden frame with clapboarding, five-bay front, two stories, gable roof, two-story pedimented tetrastyle entrance porch with large Doric columns and delicate railing at upper level. Built by Major Peter Walton in 1854. 1 ext. photo (1936); 1 data page (1936).

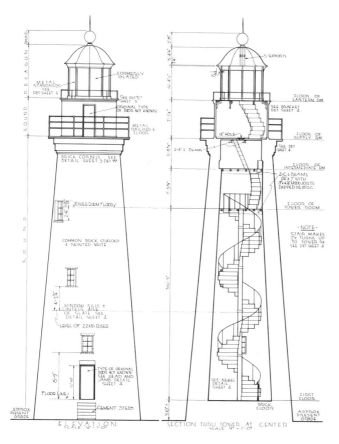

Point Isabel Lighthouse, Port Isabel/Zeb Rike, Del. 1936

PORT ISABEL   Cameron County (31)

Point Isabel Lighthouse (TEX-33-AB-1)
20 miles NE. of Brownsville

Brick, tower wall 8′ thick at base and 20′ in diameter; 88′ above mean high water level, with brick walls 4′ thick at the top of the tower. Floor of lantern is of soapstone. Lantern was reached by an iron spiral stair from frame four-room keeper's dwelling below. Along with the building of the lighthouse in 1852 went the setting up of the Brazos Beacon Light on the tip of Padre Island. Port Isabel was originally called Point Isabel. It became a port of entry between 1849-50 for increasing westbound traffic to California and inland Texas. Point Isabel Light was discontinued in 1905, but the structure has been preserved as a State Park. 4 sheets (meas. 1934, drawn 1936, including site plan, plans, elevation, sections, details); 3 ext. photos (1934), 2 int. photos (1934); 1 data page (1934).

POST VICINITY Garza County (85)

"U Lazy S" Carriage, Saddle, and Harness House (See LUB-BOCK, Lubbock County)

POTH VICINITY Wilson County (247)

Beauregard Ranch Buildings (TEX-310)
5 miles S. of Poth, not easily accessible

Fieldstone, several one-story gabled structures include a laundry and two cottages, a stone barn, and a hip-roofed smokehouse. Toutant Beauregard began construction with slave labor in 1858. The work was abandoned at the beginning of the Civil War and never resumed. 4 ext. photos (1936), 2 ext. photos of barn (1936), and 1 ext. photo of smokehouse (1936).

PRESIDIO VICINITY Presidio County (189)

Fort Leaton (TEX-3103)
4 miles SE. of Presidio between Farm Road 170 and the Rio Grande

Adobe, 141' x 202' overall, one story, flat-roofed vega construction, unglazed grilled or shuttered openings in walls 19" to 42" thick. Originally 37 rooms surrounded a patio courtyard. One outbuilding, a chapel, was still standing in 1936. Built c. 1848 by Ben Leaton as a private "baronial" fortress protecting his holdings and the trade routes through the area, it became unofficial headquarters of U. S. Army troops patrolling the border. The site may have been occupied by a Spanish mission as early as 1684. Owned and undergoing restoration by the Texas Parks and Wildlife Department. 6 sheets (1936, including site plan, plan, elevations, section, and details) ; 9 ext. photos (1936, including 1 of chapel), 7 int. photos (1936) ; 2 data pages (1936). NR.

QUIHI VICINITY   Medina County (163)

Boehle, Louis, House (TEX-33-A-18)
Quihi Road

Stone and stucco, board and shingles; 86′ x 29′ overall; one and two stories, gable roof. Following European precedent, the living quarters and stable are separated by a narrow passage and connected by a second story accessible only by exterior stairs. Built 1865. Ruinous. 2 sheets (1934, including site plan, plan, elevations, section, details) ; 6 ext. photos (1934) ; 1 data page (1934).

Schorobiny Houses 1 and 2 (TEX-371)
2 miles S. of Quihi

Similar adjacent houses. Stone and stucco, one-and-a-half stories, gable roof extends over front porches, stone chimneys and fenestration differ in each house. Built by Rudolph von Schorobiny in the early 1850's. Both houses are abandoned and ruinous. 5 ext. photos (1936), 2 int. photos (1936) ; 2 data pages (1936).

RIO GRANDE CITY   Starr County (214)

Davis, Henry Clay, House (TEX-33-Ab-4)
Gone. Formerly on Britton Avenue.

Brick, 40′1″ x 36′4″, two stories, hip roof abuts east gabled facade. Two-story wooden gallery around north and west sides. A number of one-story outbuildings were part of the complex. Built 1848 by the founder of Rio Grande City. 6 sheets (1937, including site plan, plans, elevations, sections, details) ; 4 ext. photos (1934), 1 int. photo (1934), 2 ext.

photos of outbuildings (1934) ; 1 data page (1934).

Old Courthouse (TEX-33-Ab-2)
Water Street at Texas Avenue

Brick, 84'3" x 27'1", two stories, hip roof, wooden balcony along entire front with access to second story by means of exterior stair. Built c. 1856. 4 sheets (1934, including site plan, plans, elevations, section, details) ; 2 ext. photos (1934) ; 1 data page (1934).

Silverio De La Peña Drugstore and Post Office, Rio Grande City/
W. Eugene George, Photo 1961

Peña, Silverio De La, Drugstore and Post Office (TEX-3136)
Main and Lopez Sts.

Brick, 38' x 82', two stories with store below and dwelling above, flat-roofed ornamental iron balcony on street facades.

Designed and built in 1886 by Heinrich Portscheller. 6 ext. photos (1962) ; 5 data pages (1962).

Ramírez, José, House (TEX-3133)
Gone. Originally at Corpus and 3rd Sts.

Brick, 32′ x 90′ (principal structure), one story, steep gable roof; 140′ x 90′ complex included patio with parallel buildings on east and west and walls on north and south. Built c. 1880. 6 ext. photos (1961) ; 4 data pages (1961).

Anthony D. Kennard House, Roans Prairie Vicinity/
Harry Starnes, Photo 1936

ROANS PRAIRIE VICINITY Grimes County (93)

Kennard, Anthony D., House (TEX-229)
Gone

Wooden frame, three-bay front, two stories, gable roof, shed-roofed porch at front and lean-to rooms at rear and one gable end. Stone chimney at other gable. Built 1832. 1 ext. photo (1936) ; 1 data page (1936).

Kennard, Mark, House (TEX-228)
Gone

Wooden frame, four-bay front, two stories, gable roof, with one-story six-column shed-roofed porch across front, lean-to built across back. Unusual "clerestory" between lean-to roofs and second-story roof. Built 1855. 1 ext. photo (1936) ; 1 data page (1936).

ROCKPORT Aransas County (4)

Mathis, T. H., House (TEX-3115)
612 S. Church St.

Wooden frame, five-bay front, one story on 7' to 8' high arched brick foundation, hip roof, rectangular plan with entrance porch with square fluted columns and pilasters, paneled and bracketed cornice. Built c. 1870. The townsite of Rockport was laid out by T. H. Mathis, J. M. Mathis, and J. M. Doughty in 1867. 5 ext. photos (1936), 2 int. photos (1936) ; 1 data page (1936) ; HABSI. NR.

ROMA Starr County (214)

Church of Our Lady of Refuge of Sinners (TEX-3135)
N. end of Main Plaza on Estrella Street

Brick tower and sandstone nave, 29' x 84', steep gable roof, spired entrance tower. Gothic Revival detail. Built 1854 from design of Father Pierre Keralum, who had studied architecture in Paris before his ordination in 1852. As a missionary priest along the Rio Grande he traveled on horseback from ranch to ranch for 20 years and perished on one of his journeys in November 1872. Only the tower of the Roma church remains to show his work, a larger nave having replaced the 1854 building in the mid-1960's. 7 ext. photos (1961); 5 data pages (1962).

Garcia, Leocadia Leandro, House (TEX-3131)
SW. corner of Main Plaza overlooking the Rio Grande

Sandstone with spatter finish lime stucco, painted, 26' x 60', two stories, flat roof. Built in the early 1850's for a widow who had fled Mexico. The ground floor was originally commercial space, with the dwelling above; the second floor partitions were later removed to provide space for dancing. 5 ext. photos (1961); 4 data pages (1961).

Manuel Guerra Residence and Store, Roma/W. Eugene George, Photo 1961

Rafael Garcia Ramírez House, Roma/W. Eugene George, Photo 1961

Guerra, Manuel, Residence and Store (TEX-3146)
W. side of Main Plaza at Hidalgo Street

Brick, 120'-square building complex, two stories, with roof pitched slightly toward rear; continuous ornamental ironwork balcony. Designed and built in 1884 by Heinrich Portscheller, German-born master mason, who came to Texas after deserting from service with Maximilian's troops in Mexico. 7 ext. photos (1962); 6 data pages (1962).

Ramírez, Rafael Garcia, House (TEX-3134)
E. side of Main Plaza at Hidalgo Street

Brick, 58' x 70', one story, flat roof with corbelled cornice. Five pairs of cypress exterior doors, each with five panels

and barred glass transom. Built c. 1880 by Heinrich Portscheller. Much remodeled upon incorporation with adjacent
hospital. 5 ext. photos (1962) ; 5 data pages (1962).

Saéns, Nestor, Store (TEX-3129)
Hidalgo Street and Juarez Alley

Brick, 62' (four-bay front) x 49', one story, flat roof, two
rooms, L-plan, classically proportioned facades, heavy paneled doors. Designed and built in 1884 by Heinrich Portscheller. 7 sheets (1961, including site plan, plan, elevations,
sections, details) ; 5 ext. photos (1961) ; 5 data pages (1962).

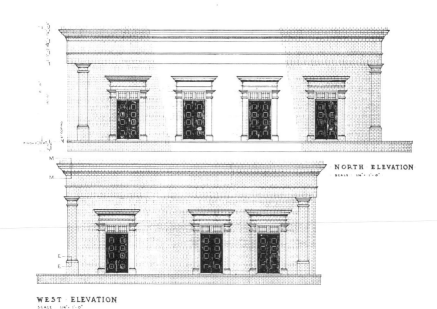

NORTH ELEVATION
SCALE 1/4" = 1'-0"

WEST ELEVATION
SCALE 1/4" = 1'-0"

Nestor Saéns Store, Roma/José G. Jiménez, Del. 1961

ROUND ROCK VICINITY

Anderson, Washington, House ("El Milagro") (TEX-336)
Tex. 79 at NE. edge of Round Rock

Limestone ashlar, one story, gable roof. Built 1852 by Washington Anderson. Much modernized since recorded. 5 ext. photos (1936), 1 int. photo (1936), 1 ext. photo of slave quarters (1936); 1 data page (1936).

Cole, Dr. J. T., House (Old Stage Stop) (TEX-3144)
One block W. of I-35 access road

Native limestone, 19' x 48', two stories, gable roof, chimneys at each gable end; railed, two-deck gallery across front. Center-hall plan. Thought to have been built in 1873 by a Mr. Lewis for J. T. Cole. Use as a stage stop questionable. 1 ext. photo (1965); 2 data pages (1965).

"El Milagro" (See *Anderson, Washington, House*)

Merrell, Captain Nelson, House (TEX-3132)
1.6 miles E. of I-35 on Tex. 79

Native limestone, 55' x 41', two stories, gable roof, chimneys at each gable end, double gallery across facade, rectangular railed cupola straddles ridge. One-story ell at rear, 32' x 31'. Built 1870-71 by A. Smith for Captain Merrell, an 1837 Texas immigrant who raised a company of Texas Rangers in 1839 to control Indian raids in the area. 6 ext. photos (1965); 4 data pages (1965). NR.

Old Stage Stop (See *Cole, Dr. J. T., House*)

ROUND TOP
Fayette County (75)

Bethlehem Lutheran Church (TEX-3124)
SW. edge of Round Top, at end of White St.

Sandstone ashlar, stuccoed, 30'6" (three-bay front) x 55', one story, gable roof with rear jerkinhead, single-stage wooden-frame belfry with louvered openings topped by pyramidal roof, massive stone buttresses on southwest wall;

Captain Nelson Merrell House, Round Rock Vicinity/
Jack E. Boucher, Photo 1965

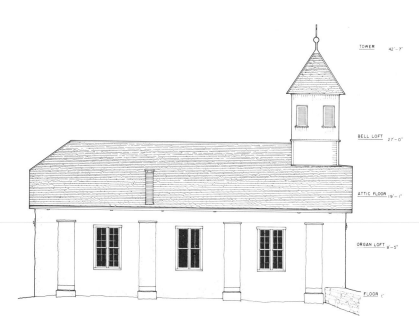

TOWER 42'-7"

BELL LOFT 27'-0"

ATTIC FLOOR 19'-1"

ORGAN LOFT 8'-5"

FLOOR 0'

Bethlehem Lutheran Church, Round Top/Roy Pledger, Del. 1972

open plan with vestibule and choir loft above at entrance, barrel-vaulted ceiling. Built 1866-67 for a German congregation by Carl Siegismund Bauer; buttresses added 1881-82. 6 sheets (1972, including site plan, plan, elevations, section, details); 2 ext. photos (1936), 4 ext. photos (1972), 2 int. photos (1936), 2 int. photos (1972); 7 data pages (1972).

Henkel, Edward, House (TEX-3196)
In NW. portion of "Henkel Square," a restoration area bordered by Live Oak and First Sts.

House museum. Frame with clapboarding, 20'3" (three-bay front) x 28'4" with 9' x 24' front porch, two stories, steeply pitched gable roof extends 3'9" beyond side wall to protect exterior stair, shed roof on porch; two-room plan on first floor, side-hall plan on second. Built c. 1851 by a German settler. 5 sheets (1972, including site plan, plans, elevations, section); 4 ext. photos (1972), 2 int. photos (1972); 5 data pages (1972).

Edward Henkel House, Round Top/Roy Pledger, Photo 1972

Edward Henkel House/Roy Pledger, Photo 1972

Kneip, Ferdinand, House (TEX-3123)
Gone

Stone and stucco, two stories, steep gable roof with one-story gabled wood addition at rear, two-story gallery across front. Built by Conrad Schuddemagen c. 1850. 3 ext. photos (1936) ; 1 data page (1936).

Rummel, Carl Wilhelm, House (TEX-3200)
Near NW. end of First St.

Sandstone ashlar (orginally stuccoed), 38′ (four-bay front) x 33′6″, one-and-a-half stories, gable roof with dormer, front porch runs length of facade; three-room plan. Built c. 1870 by a German settler. 5 sheets (1972, including site plan, plans, elevations, section) ; 3 ext. photos (1972), 3 int. photos (1972) ; 5 data pages (1972).

Ferdinand Kneip House, Round Top/Harry Starnes, Photo 1936

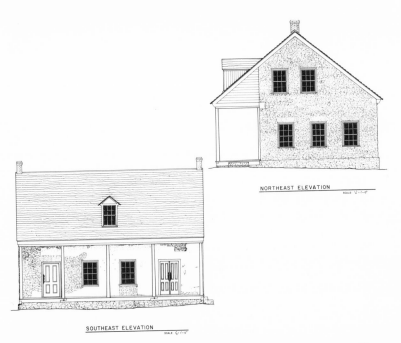

NORTHEAST ELEVATION

SOUTHEAST ELEVATION

Carl Wilhelm Rummel House, Round Top/Hans W. von Ross, Del. 1972

Carl Wilhelm Rummel House/Roy Pledger, Photo 1972

Wantke-Pochmann House (TEX-3188)
SW. corner White and Third Sts.

Rubble masonry (originally plastered), 30′ (three-bay front) x 19′, one story, gable roof; two-room plan. Built c. 1863 by a German settler as a workshop for manufacture of pipe organs, at times used for living quarters. 3 sheets (1972, including site plan, plans, elevations, sections) ; 2 ext. photos (1972), 2 int. photos (1972) ; 4 data pages (1972).

Zapp-Von Rosenberg House (TEX-3252)
"Henkel Square" restoration area

Museum. Frame with clapboarding, 43′ (five-bay front) x 32′, one story, gable roof with lesser pitch over front and rear; dog-trot plan modified by corner rooms which enclose ends of the porches. Built c. 1875 by a German settler. 2 ext. photos (1972) ; 4 data pages (1972).

Wantke-Pochmann House, Round Top/Roy Pledger, Photo 1972

SALADO VICINITY   Bell County (14)

Robertson, E. Sterling C., Plantation House (TEX-394)
1 mile S. of Salado via W. access road to I-35

Wooden frame with clapboarding, 51′5″ x 55′11″, two stories,
hip roof, with two-tiered gabled entry porch and galleries on
center front, and with two-story corner pavilions. Robertson
settled on this vast plantation in 1852 and built his house c.
1856. It is probably the most complete surviving example
of a Texas plantation complex. HABS records also include
stone, one-story dining-kitchen-laundry unit connected to
main house by a passageway; stone, one-story slave quarters,
18′ x 100′; stone and wooden frame barn 48′7″ x 50′4″. 16
sheets (1936, including site plan, plans, elevations, details of

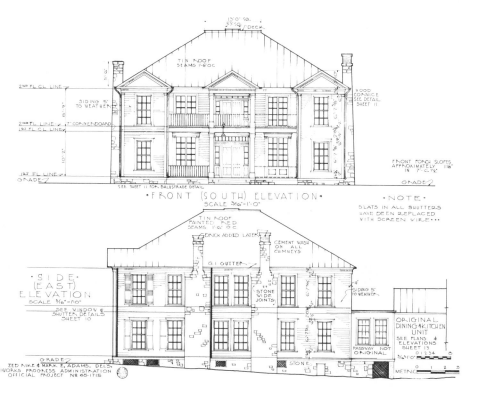

Sterling C. Robertson Plantation House, Salado Vicinity/
Zeb Rike and Mark E. Adams, Del. 1936

house, kitchen-laundry unit, slave quarters and barn); 4 ext.
photos (1936), 2 int. photos (1936), 2 ext. photos of slave
quarters (1936), 2 ext. photos of barn (1936); 3 data pages
(1937).

"Shady Villa" (Stagecoach Inn) (TEX-395)
East access road to I-35

Wooden frame with clapboarding, five-bay front, two stories,
gable roof, two-tiered front gallery. Rectangular plan. Built
1858 at a crossroads of the Chisholm Trail and the Old Military Road. Later the Overland Stage Line ran nearby, and
now the Interstate highway is close. The Inn has been
restored and its dining rooms again serve travelers. 4 ext.
photos (1936), 1 int. photo (1936); 1 data page (1937).

Stagecoach Inn (See *"Shady Villa"*)

183

NOTE: A number of San Antonio structures not recorded below have been recorded solely on HABS Inventory forms. They are listed on pages 237-240.

The Alamo (Mission San Antonio de Valero) (TEX-318)
Alamo Plaza

Museum. Limestone church, 75' x 106', vaulted roof, Latin cross plan, richly carved stonework surrounds arched entrance with Corinthianesque pilasters, shell-arched niches. The profile of the pediment dates from U.S. Army construction in 1850. The remaining adjacent convent is a limestone, one-story, 20' x 190' row of rooms with an arcade along the east side. The walls remain from a mission church begun in 1744, still under construction in 1777 and probably never completed because of the decline in the Indian population at the mission. About 1803 a company of soldiers from the Pueblo de San Jose y Santiago del Alamo occupied the secularized mission and gave it the name "Alamo." In 1835 Mexican General Cos fortified the church by pulling down the arches to build an inclined plane to move cannon to the top of the walls. After defeating Cos, Texan forces occupied the ruin until they were besieged and slaughtered by Santa Anna in March 1836. The martyrdom of Travis, Bowie, Crockett, Bonham and their fellow defenders in the cause of Texas Independence has made the Alamo the most revered historic site in Texas. Restoration of the church and convent was done in 1850 when the army leased them for quartermaster stores, in 1878 for private wholesale grocery warehousing and in 1921-22 by the state of Texas, the site having been acquired by legislative action of 1905. 17 sheets (1961, including site plan, plans, elevations, sections, details) ; 15 ext. photos (1936), 5 ext. photos (1961), 6 int. photos (1961) ; 3 data pages (1936), 12 data pages (1968*). HABSI. NHL, NR.

WEST ELEVATION

- EAST - ELEVATION -

The Alamo, San Antonio/José Jiménez and James Emmrich, Del. 1961

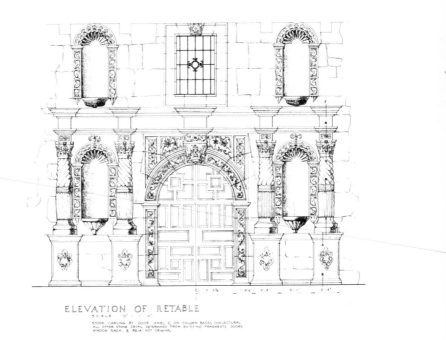

ELEVATION OF RETABLE

The Alamo/W. Eugene George, Jr., Del. 1961

Ernst H. Altgelt House, San Antonio/Jack E. Boucher, Photo 1961

Alamo Roman and Portland Cement Company Building (TEX-3173)
N. St. Mary's Street in Brackenridge Park

Limestone rectangular kilns with cylindrical brick chimney. The quarry which supplied raw material for cement manufacture has been transformed into a sunken garden and the ruinous kilns support an observation platform. Cement production here began in 1880 at the rate of ten barrels per day; the expanding company moved from this site in 1908. 4 sheets (1968*, including site plan, plans, elevations); 6 data pages (1968*). HABSI.

Altgelt, Ernst H., House (George P. Isbell House) (TEX-3147)
226 King William St.

Limestone, rough-hewn ashlar, 28' (two-bay front) x 40',

two stories, low-pitched gable roof, round-arched entrance in gable end, wood-railed balcony at second-story door and window, two-story veranda at rear and side. Altgelt was the developer of the fine residential neighborhood of King William Street, which he named for Wilhelm I of Prussia. He died in 1878 before the house was completed. 3 ext. photos (1961); 5 data pages (1963). HABSI. NR (in King William Historic District).

Argyle House (TEX-36)
934 Patterson at Argyle—Alamo Heights

Stone and wood, five-bay front, three stories, gable roof. An original stone, two-story, cross-plan structure was built in 1859; the third story, wood facade, and flat-roofed portico are late 19th-century additions which adapted "the Argyle" for use as a hotel from 1893 to 1940. It is now a private club. 7 ext. photos (1936); 1 data page (1936).

Ball House (TEX-3151)
120 King William St.

Stone, stuccoed, 36' x 36', gable roof extended over porch across front. A typical example of a simple central Texas dwelling of the mid-19th century. Built c. 1856 for John Ball; John H. Camp, architect and builder. 1 ext. photo (1961); 4 data pages (1964). NR (in King William Historic District).

Bexar County Courthouse (TEX-3174)
Main Plaza (20 Dolorosa St.)

Pecos red sandstone above high red granite basement, rock-faced ashlar, 140' x 400', hip roof, north entrance recessed in broad segmental arch supporting a colonnade which wraps around cylindrical buttressing towerlets; these are flanked by tall square towers, the west one topped by a pyramid of green tile, the taller east tower ends in a beehive form of red tile. Romanesque Revival detail. Built 1891-96. Architect was James Riely Gordon, winner of 1891 competition. Extensive additions at the rear were made in 1914-15 and 1926-28, when all of the interiors were redesigned. 2 sheets (1968*, plans and elevation); 6 ext. photos (1968*); 7 data pages (1968*); HABSI.

Bexar County Courthouse, San Antonio/Dewey G. Mears, Photo 1968

Boelhauwe, Joseph, House (TEX-3153)
Gone. Formerly 321 N. Alamo.

Limestone and stuccoed brick, 40′ (three-bay front) x 50′, one story, gable roofs concealed by front parapet with bracketed cornice, front porch with alternating narrow and wide column spacing, rope moldings and intricate jigsawn ornament including central Masonic emblems over arches of porch. Built in 1876-77 by Benjamin Grossenbacher, a skilled German cabinet maker. In 1886 his widow married Joseph Boelhauwe, a builder, who enlarged the house at the rear. 2 ext. photos (1961) ; 4 data pages (1963) ; HABSI.

Casa Villita (See *Dashiell, Colonel Jeremiah Y., House*)

Concepción Mission (See *Mission Nuestra Señora de la Purísima Concepción de Acuña*)

Cos House (TEX-33-A-6)
513 Paseo de la Villita

Stone, stuccoed, 15'11" x 53'8", one story, gable roof, three rooms with separate entrance doors. Canvas ceilings. Erected before 1835. Reputed to be the site of the surrender of Mexican General Martin P. de Cos to Texas Revolutionary General Edward Burleson in December 1835. 2 sheets (1934, including site plan, plans, elevations, section) ; 2 ext. photos (1934), 1 int. photo (1934) ; 1 data page (1934). NR (in La Villita Historic District).

Dashiell, Colonel Jeremiah Y., House (Casa Villita) (TEX-3169)
511 Paseo de la Villita

Limestone, stuccoed and painted, one story with basement, steep hip roof, porch across front. The site slopes to the San Antonio River, making the basement a full story opening to the rear garden. Built c. 1850. Restored and occupied by the San Antonio Conservation Society. 7 sheets (1968*, including plans, elevations, section, details) ; 3 ext. photos (1968*), 2 int. photos (1968*), 3 ext. photos (1969*) ; 3 data pages (1968*), 6 data pages (1969*) ; HABSI. NR (in La Villita Historic District).

Denman House (See *Lewis, Nat., House*)

Des Mazieres, Francis Louis, Store Building and House (TEX-33-A-2)
Gone. Martinez and South Alamo Sts.

Lime and gravel concrete, stuccoed, two stories; hipped-roof store 20' (four-bay front) x 50'; gabled-roof residence 40' (four-bay front) x 30'; with plain, two-story galleries on the street facade of store, but ornamental galleries on house. The store at South Alamo and Martinez Streets was built in 1853 and the adjacent house in 1854. Mr. Kampman was the stonemason. 5 sheets (1934, including plans, elevations, sections, details) ; 5 ext. photos (1934) ; 2 data pages (1934, revised 1936).

Devine, Judge Thomas J., House (TEX-332)
Gone

Limestone and brick, one story, hip roof, 75' seven-bay porch across front with arched treatment between square columns. U-plan. Interiors with 16' ceilings and 10' door heights. Built c. 1850 for Judge Thomas J. Devine, a prominent lawyer and Commissioner of the Confederacy. Later additions. 6 ext. photos (1936), 1 int. photo (1936) ; 1 data page (1937).

Espada Aqueduct (TEX-322)
Espada Road and Piedra Creek

Stone arches span Piedra Creek to carry irrigation water from the San Antonio River to fields of the Mission San Francisco de la Espada. Built 1731 under the direction of the Franciscan Friars of the Mission. 5 photos (1936) show double arched aqueduct and embankment; 1 data page (1937). NR.

Espada Mission (See *Mission San Francisco de la Espada*)

French Mansard House (See *Kingsley, Dr. B. F., House*)

Isbell, George P., House (See *Altgelt, Ernst H., House*)

Kampmann, John, House (TEX-396)
Gone

Limestone, stuccoed, one story and basement, gabled ell plan, porch across front. Interesting stables with living quarters above. Built in mid-19th century with later additions. 6 ext. photos (1936), 5 int. photos (1936), 2 photos of stable (1936) ; 2 data pages (1937).

Kingsley, Dr. B. F., House (French Mansard House) (TEX-33-A-3)
Gone. Formerly 408 Elm St.

Limestone, stuccoed, 42' (three-bay front) x 46', two stories, with one-story rear additions, concave mansard roof with projecting pavilion above front entrance, segmental-arched dormers, heavily molded and paneled entrance doors. This house is believed to have been at least 30 years old when bought in 1890 by Dr. Kingsley, who used a picture of the house in his advertisements. 7 sheets (1934, including plans, elevations, section, details) ; 4 ext. photos (1934) ; 1 data page (1934).

Lege, Charles L., House (Santleben House) (TEX-3172)
Gone. Formerly 533 Elmira St.

Stone, stuccoed, 49′ (seven-bay front) x 76′, one story, hip roof, square-columned gallery across front and parts of each end. Two French doors with side lights and transom compose the original front entrance. Built c. 1855. 4 sheets (1968*, including plan, elevations, details). HABSI.

Lewis, Nat., House (Denman House) (TEX-393)
Gone. Originally 112 Lexington.

Native limestone, five-bay front, two stories, gabled rectangle with intersecting gable above one-story, flat-roofed entrance porch. Side, second-story balconies, louvered shutters. Rear ell with slave quarters and smokehouse beyond. Built before 1850. 8 ext. photos (1936, including 2 of stone slave quarters and smokehouse) ; 1 data page (1937).

Menger Hotel (TEX-35)
Alamo Plaza

Limestone and stucco, three and four stories, landscaped courtyards. A two-story facade of classic symmetry characterized the Menger Hotel when it opened in 1859. Addition of a third floor and expansion toward the north obscure but do not completely conceal the original structure. 17 ext. photos (1936) ; 2 data pages (1936).

Mission Nuestra Señora de la Purísima Concepción de Acuña (Concepción Mission) (TEX-319)
807 Mission Rd.

Museum and church. Tufa (a soft, porous limestone, easily quarried and shaped, but becoming hard upon exposure to air), 59′ (three-bay front) x 93′, two stories, cruciform, walls 3′ to 4′ thick, vaulted roof of solid stone; twin square western towers, domed crossing, entrance door framed by carved stone pilasters supporting steep triangular pediment. The mission was established at its present site in 1731;

Menger Hotel, San Antonio/Arthur Stewart, Photo 1936

the stone buildings were under construction in 1743, and the
church was dedicated by 1755. Although it suffered from
periods of neglect in the 19th century, the original vault and
dome construction have remained intact, as has part of the
convent; and the church, having again its original appearance of 1731, is well maintained as a place of regular worship.
Records indicate the facade was once plastered and frescoed
with yellow and orange squares having red and blue quatre-
foils and crosses. Builders were the Franciscan friars and
mission Indians. 5 sheets (1934, including plans, elevations,
sections, details); 11 ext. photos (1936), 2 ext. photos of
old living quarters (1936), 1 ext. photo courtyard (1936);
3 data pages (1937), 7 data pages (1969*). HABSI. NHL,
NR.

ELEVATION of TOWER
SCALE: ¼" = 1'-0"

WEST ELEVATION
SCALE: 1/16" = 1'-0"

SECTION "A-A"
SCALE: 1/16" = 1'-0"

NORTH ELEVATION
SCALE: 1/16" = 1'-0"

Mission Concepción, San Antonio/Welton Cook, Del. 1934

Mission San Antonio de Valero (See *"The Alamo"*)

Mission San Francisco de la Espada (Espada Mission)
(TEX-320)
Espada Road

Museum and church. Rubble stone, one story, 63' x 38', flat
roof supported by wooden beams; the facade is notable for
the upper arched openings where the bells are hung and for
the entrance arch, its voussoirs incorrectly reassembled in
a restoration. Spanish colonial. Like the other San Antonio
missions, Espada was a compound of Indian dwellings, work-
rooms, granary, convent and church with a central plaza
and surrounding farmlands. The church was completed in
1856, 25 years after the founding of the mission at this
site. It survived a later and larger church which was poorly

193

built. By 1858 only the facade was left standing, but the little church was rebuilt by Father Francis Boucher, who served in it until 1907. In 1909 it was again restored without the north transept. There has been considerable restoration and reconstruction of auxiliary structures at Espada in recent years. 4 sheets (1934, including site plan of entire mission, plan of church, elevations, details of entrance) ; 20 ext. photos (1936) ; 2 data pages (1936). HABSI. NR.

Mission San José y San Miguel de Aguayo (San José Mission) (TEX-333)
6539 San José

National Historic Site. Museum, church. Limestone, one and two stories. The church, about 40' x 80', is the principal structure of the mission complex with a richly carved stone facade, flanked by square towers (only the south tower is complete), a vaulted roof with a dome over the crossing, and a famous "rose window" in the sacristy or chapel. The walls and structural arches of a two-story friary or "convento" are attached at the rear of the church. In its present state, the mission compound is a square surrounded by restored ramparts suggesting the fortified character of the original. These buildings, about 18' wide, contain flat-roofed apartments which open toward the compound and present blank walls to the outside except for fortified gates on each side. A three-bay buttressed granary occupies the northwest corner of the ramparts. The mission of San José was founded in 1720 and established at its present site about 1739. The church was under construction in 1768 under the supervision of Father Pedro Ramirez de Arellano. Its beauty and the construction of the fortifications were universally admired by 18th-century visitors. Irregular occupancy in the 19th century brought ruin to parts of the compound and parts of the church collapsed in 1868, 1874 and 1928. Restoration was extensive in 1934-36 and in 1947-52. The church was rededicated in April 1937. HABS records have been gathered on both the entire mission complex and on the individual components. Mission complex: 6 sheets (1934, including plans, sections and elevations before restoration, details of door and rose window) ; 30 ext. photos (1936), 3 int. photos (1936) ; 9 data pages (1936), 11 data pages

Mission San José, San Antonio/Arthur Stewart, Photo 1936

(1968*). Church: 6 data pages (1968*). Chapel: 3 data pages (1968*). Convent: 3 data pages (1968*). Granary: 3 data pages (1968*). Ramparts and Indian dwellings: 5 data pages (1968*). HABSI.

Mission San Juan Capistrano (San Juan Capistrano Mission) (TEX-321)
Berg's Mill—Graf Road

Museum and church. Rubble, one story, 20′ x 101′ chapel, present flat roof replaces original thatched gable, segmental relieving arches in long east wall, bells hang in superimposed arches above entrance at north end of east facade. Spanish colonial. A convent and Indian habitations are gabled rectangular structures. The habitations were largely rebuilt in 1968 with thatched roofs. The chapel was completed by 1756; decline in Indian population prevented completion of a more ambitious mission church, the foundations of which are still extant. Only intermittently occupied in the 19th century and sometimes roofless, the chapel was reconstructed for rededication in January 1909. 2 sheets (1934, including plan and elevations of entire mission complex as it existed then); 17 ext. photos (1936); 3 data pages (1969*). In addition, material has been recorded on the individual components as follows: Chapel: 3 data pages (1969*). Convent: 2 data pages (1969*). Habitation A: 2 data pages (1969*). Habitation B: 2 data pages (1969*). HABSI. NR.

Mitchell-Ogé House, San Antonio/Larry Hermsen, Del. 1968

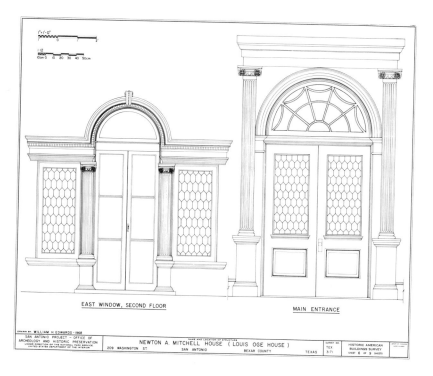

EAST WINDOW, SECOND FLOOR

MAIN ENTRANCE

Mitchell-Ogé House/William H. Edwards, Del. 1968

Mitchell-Ogé House (TEX-3171)
209 Washington St.

Limestone, stuccoed, 52′3″ (five-bay front) x 30′, two stories and raised basement, hip roof with flat central deck; cornice breaks over central bay of two-story front gallery with pediment. Center-hall plan. Built 1859 for Newton A. Mitchell and originally a one-story Classic Revival design. The present appearance dates from remodeling c. 1882 for Louis Ogé, an Alsatian immigrant, Texas Ranger, Indian fighter and rancher who retired to San Antonio in 1881. 9 sheets (1968*, including site plan, plans, elevations, section, details); 3 ext. photos (1968*); 12 data pages (1968*). HABSI. NR (in King William Historic District).

Navarro, José Antonio, House (TEX-3148)
228 S. Laredo St.

Museum. Limestone, stuccoed, one story, 40' x 48', gable roof extending over porch across front. L-plan. Separate kitchen, 36' x 18'. Built c. 1840 as the home of José Antonio Navarro, a signer of the Texas Declaration of Independence. Restored with adjacent store by the San Antonio Conservation Society. 1 ext. photo (1961); 6 data pages (1963). NR.

Navarro, José Antonio, Store (TEX-317) (See also TEX-3148)
232 S. Laredo at W. Nueva St.

Museum. Limestone, stuccoed, with exposed quoins, 24'8" x 21'5", two stories, hip roof, exterior stair at rear. Built c. 1850 as the office of José Antonio Navarro, whose house is adjacent. 3 sheets (1936, including plans, elevations, details); 2 ext. photos (1936), 1 ext. photo (1961); 1 data page (1937). NR.

José Antonio Navarro Store, San Antonio/Arthur Stewart, Photo 1936

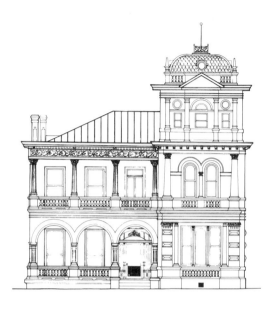

Norton-Polk-Mathis House, San Antonio/Charles W. Barrow, Jr., Del. 1969

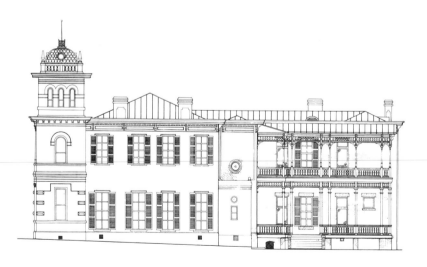

Norton-Polk-Mathis House/Charles W. Barrow, Jr., Del. 1969

Norton-Polk-Mathis House (TEX-3225)
401 King William St.

Ashlar and brick, 27'6" x 92'2", two stories, shallow hip roof, two-tiered front portico with arches on first-floor level, columns above, three-story tower at northeast corner, mansard roof. First floor built 1876 for Russell C. Norton, San Antonio merchant. In 1882 the property was acquired by Edward Polk, who added a rear two-story brick wing with a wooden gallery, and then the three-story tower and porch. Interior paneling, molding and carving were accented by ornate lock plates and door knobs. Extensively restored by Walter Nold Mathis by 1967. 12 sheets (1969*, including plans, elevations, details). HABSI. NR (in King William Historic District).

O. Henry House (William Sydney Porter House) (TEX-325)
Lone Star Brewery, 600 Lone Star Blvd.

Adobe, stuccoed, one story, gable roof. This small, three-room house was built c. 1855. William Sydney Porter, whose short stories were written under the name of O. Henry, rented the house 1894-95. 3 ext. photos (1936) ; 1 data page (1936).

Porter, William Sydney, House (See *O. Henry House*)

Ruiz, Francisco, House (TEX-3117)
Witte Museum, 3801 Broadway, Brackenridge Park. (Formerly on Dolorosa St.)

Museum meeting room. Adobe, with pine, cypress, and oak wood work, one story, hip roof, quoins, front porch. Said to date from 1745. Used at one time by Col. Ruiz, one of the signers of the Declaration of Texas Independence. Moved from Dolorosa Street and reconstructed in 1943. 2 ext. photos (1936) ; 1 data page (1937).

Saint Mark's Episcopal Church (TEX-33)
307 E. Pecan St.

Limestone ashlar, steep gable roof over nave, breaking to lesser pitch over the aisles ; low buttresses ; stone tracery in segmental pointed-arched windows. Unusual breadth and lightness in interior construction. Gothic Revival. Architect, Richard Upjohn. Construction began with cornerstone laying on December 22, 1859. Walls had reached a height of seven feet at the outbreak of the Civil War, which halted all work until March 1873. The first services in the completed church were held on Easter Sunday, 1875. 4 ext. photos (1936); 3 data pages (1936); HABSI.

San Fernando Cathedral (TEX-34)
Main Plaza (115 Main Ave.)

Cut limestone, 75' x 180', six-bay plan plus chancel, crossing and apse, gabled nave, dome over crossing, twin square towers at the corners of the east facade, lancet aisle windows, wheel windows in east and west gables. Gothic Revival. Although the first foundation stone was laid in 1734, it was 15 years later that the church of San Fernando was sufficiently complete for official blessing. Structurally unsound and poorly maintained, the church suffered a series of collapses and a severe fire. A cornerstone for a new church was laid in 1859 and again in 1868 after the interruption of the Civil War. Francis Giraud was architect of the new San Fernando Cathedral, which was large enough to surround the old building while services continued uninterrupted. Portions of the old church were incorporated in the chancel of the new, which was consecrated in October 1873. 1 ext. photo (before 1866), 6 ext. photos (1936), 1 ext. photo (1968*), 3 int. photos (1968*); 2 data pages (1937), 12 data pages (1969*); HABSI.

San José Mission (See *Mission San José y San Miguel de Aguayo*)

San Juan Capistrano Mission (See *Mission San Juan Capistrano*)

Santleben House (See *Lege, Charles L., House*)

Seng, Magnus, House (TEX-33-A-15)
Gone

Adobe, 76'6" long, one story, hip roof, linear five-room plan with remains of parallel five-room lean-to. Typical adobe construction. Built c. 1842. 3 sheets (1936, including site plan, plan, elevations, details) ; 2 ext. photos (1934), 3 int. photos (1936) ; 1 data page (1937).

Steves, Edward, House ("Steves Homestead") (TEX-3150) 509 King William St.

Museum. Limestone with smooth rustication, 50′ x 55′, two-and-a-half stories, concave mansard roof with iron lace cresting, arched dormers, one-story porch across front with decorative wood arches, turned balustrade at the roof, bracketed cornices. L-plan. Central hall with open stair, paneled octagonal newel post. 13′ ceiling in parlor, office, sitting room and dining room, fresco on parlor ceiling. Built 1876; architect, Alfred Giles; builders, John H. Kampmann and Anthony Earhart. Edward Steves was the proprietor of a very successful lumber yard, which probably explains the rich interior and exterior millwork. 5 ext. photos (1961), 2 int. photos (1961) ; 6 data pages (1963) ; HABSI. NR (in King William Historic District).

Edward Steves House, San Antonio/Jack E. Boucher, Photo 1961

Twohig, John, House (TEX-31)
Witte Museum, 3801 Broadway, Brackenridge Park

Limestone ashlar, four-bay front, hip roof. The home of an Irish-born Texas patriot, suffering imprisonment by Mexican captors in 1842, but living to become a successful banker before his death in 1891. The house was moved in 1941 to the Museum and extensively restored. 4 ext. photos (1936); 1 data page (1936).

Uhl, Gustave, Store (TEX-315)
721 Avenue E

Limestone and stucco, one story, gable roof, with lean-to addition. Built as a residence in two parts, with differing roof pitches, and occupied as both house and store until Uhl moved his family to an adjacent house (TEX-316) in 1890. 6 ext. photos (1936), 1 int. photo (1936); 1 data page (1936); HABSI.

Uhl, Gustave, House (TEX-316)
Gone

Limestone and stucco, five-bay front, one story, gable roof extending over porch across front. Built c. 1855. Purchased by Uhl in 1890 from Jacob D. Wurzbach. 5 ext. photos (1936); 1 data page (1936).

United States San Antonio Arsenal Depot Complex (TEX-3188)
Bounded by Flores Street on W., Arsenal Street on S., private property on N., and San Antonio River on E.

In 1858 San Antonio was designated the permanent location for the United States Arsenal, Department of Texas. The arsenal had previously been housed in temporary quarters (at first in the Alamo complex), but with a permanent designation, new land was purchased and building operations begun. In November 1859 work was started on the Arsenal Office Building, which was completed prior to the Civil War. The war interrupted the operation so drastically that new construction was not resumed until 1871. By 1882 there were five permanent buildings. New additions to the complex continued until 1916, by which time there were 44 buildings.

After the operation was transferred to the Red River Arsenal, the San Antonio operation decreased, and in 1947 all arsenal functions at the site ceased. The grounds and buildings have been converted to other government uses. NR. In addition to 8 data pages (1968*) on the general history of the arsenal, HABS has recorded the following individual structures:

U.S. San Antonio Arsenal Commanding Officer's Quarters (TEX-3177)

Limestone ashlar, about 60' (seven-bay front) x 75', two stories, hip roof, bracketed cornice, extensive two-story porches, large bay windows. Center hall plan, with open stair and paneled walnut newel post, stamped metal ceilings, coal-burning fireplaces. Built 1883-86. Originally had a mansard roof. Located on the northeastern quarter of the Arsenal property, the Commanding Officer's Quarters has always served as the "front yard" of the Arsenal. 8 ext. photos (1968*); 6 data pages (1968*). HABSI.

U.S. San Antonio Arsenal Magazine (TEX-3167)

Local limestone coursed ashlar, 30' x 110', one story, gable roof over a masonry barrel vault, rectangular plan. Magazine begun in 1860, not completed until after the War between the States. The work the Confederates had done to finish the Magazine at the outbreak of the war was done with soft rock. In 1868 that part was torn out and replaced with hard rock, as was originally intended. 3 sheets (1968*, including plans, elevations, details); 4 ext. photos (1968*). HABSI.

U.S. San Antonio Arsenal Office Building (TEX-3176)

Local limestone ashlar, 28' x 62', one story, gable roof, open galleries along east and west sides have been enclosed in recent times. Central corridor flanked by offices. Built 1859-60 as the first permanent military building erected in Texas by the U.S. Government. Other governmental functions continue to use the building for its original purpose as office space. 6 data pages (1968*). HABSI.

U.S. San Antonio Arsenal Servants' Quarters (TEX-3179)

Limestone, stuccoed, 19' x 41' ell plan, two stories, low-pitched hip roof. When the U.S. Army purchased the Arsenal site in December 1858, it included the homestead of Dr. James M. Devine with a fine house which became the Commanding Officer's Quarters. This servants' quarters, built c. 1855, is the only surviving structure of the outbuildings of which it was originally a part. 2 ext. photos (1968*); 4 data pages (1968*). HABSI.

U.S. San Antonio Arsenal Stable (TEX-3178)

Limestone ashlar, 31' x 60', two stories, low-pitched gable roof, segmental arched door openings now filled with masonry. Built 1873-74. 5 data pages (1968*). HABSI.

U.S. San Antonio Arsenal Storehouse (TEX-3168)

Limestone ashlar, 43' x 155', two stories, hip roof, segmental arched openings with quoined jambs and voussoirs. Built 1883. Remodeled for office use since 1947. 5 ext. photos (1968*); 5 data pages (1968*). HABSI.

Ursuline Academy (TEX-32)
300 Augusta St.

A small group of Ursuline nuns from New Orleans and Galveston arrived in San Antonio in September 1851 to found a school for girls which opened on November 3rd. The first academic building was completed by 1852 and may be assumed to be the work of Jules Poinsard, a native of France who advertised himself as an architect and contractor experienced in pisé work, the rammed earth type of construction used here. Later buildings are attributed to Father C. M. Dubuis in 1854 and Francis Giraud in 1870. The French origins of the nuns and their architects may have imparted some subtle French qualities to the construction. In 1965 the Ursuline Academy vacated the old buildings and moved to a new location. 21 sheets (1968*, including site plan, plans, elevations, sections, details); 6 ext. photos (1936, primarily of original academy building), 8 ext. photos (1961, including priest's house) ; 2 data pages (1937), 9 data pages (1968*). HABSI. NR.

In addition to the above records on the Academy complex, HABS has records on the individual buildings as follows:

Academy building

Stuccoed pisé, 28'6" x 80', two stories, original hip roof now gabled, two-story galleries on long north and south sides, louvered shutters, bell cupola. Built 1851-52 by Jules Poinsard. 13 ext. photos (1968*) ; 7 data pages (1968*). HABSI.

Academy building addition

Limestone rubble, 68' x 45', two stories with one-story wing, hip roof with tiny gabled dormers. Built 1853-54 and attributed to Father C. M. Dubuis. 2 ext. photos (1968*) ; 6 data pages (1968*). HABSI.

Chapel

Limestone, 64' x 95', cross surmounts gabled parapet, lancet arched stained glass windows. The plan has a small nave, a larger west transept with rear balcony and a very shallow two-story east transept or oratory. The tongue-and-groove ceilings date from about 1900 and take a gambrel form over the large transept and an inverted pyramid pendant at the crossing. Built 1868-70. 2 int. photos (1968*) ; 4 data pages (1968*). HABSI.

Dormitory building

Limestone rubble, 46' x 152' with west end cut obliquely to conform to street, two stories, hip roof with square central clock tower with only three clock faces and blank north face, two-story gallery on north and east with square columns and ornamented box capitals. Begun in 1866 to provide housing for boarding students. Attributed to Francis Giraud, Jr. 5 ext. photos (1968*) ; 4 data pages (1968*). HABSI.

Priest's house

Dressed limestone, 68' x 71', two stories, gable roofs with ornamental parapets at end walls, dormer faces are extensions of stone facade, sheet metal balustrade above cornice has repeated trefoil arch. Built c. 1882-85. 3 ext. photos (1968*); 4 data pages (1968*). HABSI.

House

Limestone, 21' x 47', two stories, gable roof, one-story porch at north. A plain house built in 1872 by John Campbell. 1 ext. photo (1968*); 4 data pages (1968*). HABSI.

House (*Laundry*)

Limestone, 70' x 40', one and two stories, gable roof, one-story lean-to porches. 6 ext. photos (1968*); 5 data pages (1968*). HABSI.

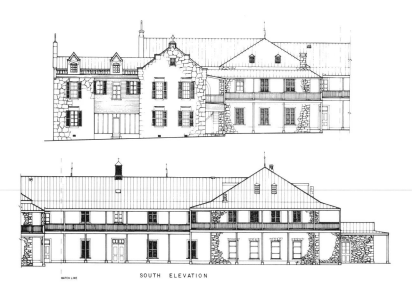

SOUTH ELEVATION

Ursuline Academy, San Antonio/Charles W. Barrow, Jr., Del. 1968

WEST ELEVATION

Ursuline Academy/Charles W. Barrow, Jr., Del. 1968

Vance, James, House (TEX-33-A-1)
Gone

Limestone, 52' x 59', two stories and basement, hip roof, six square columns at front and rear two-story galleries, ornamental iron railings at front, wood railings at rear, dentil moulding at cornice. Center-hall plan, reception room 17' x 35'. Greek Revival. Completed 1859. Attributed to John Fries, architect. James Vance and his brother John were wealthy merchants and bankers. 10 sheets (1934, including plot plan, plans, elevations, sections, details); 3 ext. photos (1934), 3 int. photos (1934, including stair, ceiling ornament and chandelier); 2 data pages (1934).

Vollrath House and Store (TEX-3152)
Gone. Formerly 712 S. Alamo St.

Limestone ashlar, 27'-square plan, two-bay front, two stories, low-pitched gable roof, two-story porch and stair at rear, wooden cantilevered balconies at front and side. This bakery with living quarters above was built in 1882 by the widow of Louis Vollrath of Hanover, Germany. 1 ext. photo (1961); 5 data pages (1964).

Wulff, Anton, House (TEX-3149)
107 King William St.

Limestone, 52' x 55', two stories above high basement, low pitched gable roof with gable end toward street; front porch has basement and first-floor decks, ornamental pointed arches in wood, and flat roof. Italianate detail in pairs of round-arched second-story windows, a circular bas relief in the gable end, and a four-story, hip-roofed entrance tower. Built 1870-72 on a three-and-one-half acre plot backing on the San Antonio River. Wulff, born in Hamburg, Germany, served several terms as an alderman and became San Antonio's first Park Commissioner. 1 ext. photo (1961); 6 data pages (1963); HABSI. NR (in King William Historic District).

SAN ANTONIO VICINITY   Bexar County (15)

Casa Vieja (TEX-323)
Blue Wing Road, 2.4 miles E. of Farm Road 1937

Limestone and stucco, 36'6" x 18', two stories, gable roof with boxed cornice; much altered by additions. Built 1848 by James L. Truehart, Texas pioneer and soldier. 5 sheets (1936, including plans, elevations, details); 4 ext. photos (1936), 1 int. photo (1936); 2 data pages (1936).

Casa Vieja Lime Kiln and Arch (TEX-324)
Blue Wing Road, 2.4 miles E. of Farm Road 1937

Limestone, two dome-shaped kilns used for burning lime for construction. Built 1848. The stone arch or viaduct permitted builders to carry lime across a creek which ran between the kilns and the building site. 2 ext. photos (1936); 1 data page (1936).

SAN AUGUSTINE   San Augustine County (203)

Blount, Colonel Stephen W., House (TEX-33-D-1)
501 E. Columbia St.

Wooden frame, 96' x 15' main stem running behind central 37' x 18' unit, other wings at rear, one story. Pedimented

Colonel Stephen W. Blount House, San Augustine/E. O. Taylor, Photo 1934

front entrance porch. Greek Revival detail includes triglyphs
and metopes at central unit cornice. Built 1839; architect,
Augustus Phelps of Brandon, Vermont. Built for Stephen
W. Blount, a signer of the Texas Declaration of Independence. Restored in 1950's by Raiford D. Stripling, architect.
4 sheets (1934, including site plan, plan, elevations, section,
details) ; 6 ext. photos (1934) ; 2 data pages (1936).

Cartright, Columbus, House (TEX-239)
SE. edge of San Augustine at end of Sharp Street

Wooden frame, one-and-a-half stories, gable roof, raised
square-columned pedimented portico over two separate front
doors ; one-story wing at one side with porch with ornamental
posts and brackets. There is some evidence that this house,
begun c. 1838, may incorporate parts of two or more houses.
1 ext. photo (1936) ; 1 data page (1936).

Cartwright, Matthew, House (TEX-238)
505 E. Main St.

Wooden frame, 42'3" (five-bay front) x 21'5", two stories, with one-story ell, 23'2" x 45'5", gable roof, one-story hip-roofed entrance porch with fluted Doric columns. Greek Revival. Built 1839 for Matthew Cartwright. An original well house and Greek Revival-detailed one-room office building also exist on the property. 5 sheets (1934, including site plan, plans, elevations, section); 5 ext. photos (1934), 3 ext. photos (1936), 2 int. photos (1936), 1 ext. photo of office (1936); 1 data page (1936). NR.

Matthew Cartwright House, San Augustine/1934

Matthew Cartwright House/Harry L. Starnes, Photo 1936

Cullen-Roberts House (TEX-237)
Congress and Market Sts.

Wooden frame, one story, pedimented tetrastyle portico on short, broad pillars across entire front of house, massive cornice. The breadth and weight of the pediment would seem more appropriate to a two-story design. Built in 1839 for Judge Ezekiel W. Cullen. Owned by Benjamin Roberts after the Civil War. In recent decades the house was purchased by Cullen's grandson, restored by Raiford L. Stripling, architect, and presented to the San Augustine Chapter of the Daughters of the Republic of Texas. 1 ext. photo (1936), 1 int. photo (1936); 1 data page (1936). NR.

Johnson, C. C., House (TEX-242)
N. end of Congress Street

Wooden frame, two stories, gable roof, rectangular plan,

inside gable-end chimney. Built by Almanzon Houston in 1850; the addition of a one-story porch along the front in late 19th-century jigsaw style has altered the character of the house considerably. 1 ext. photo (1936); 1 data page (1936).

SAN AUGUSTINE VICINITY
San Augustine County (203)

Garrett, William, Plantation House (TEX-33-D-2)
2 miles W. of San Augustine on Tex. 21

Wooden frame, 66'2" (five-bay front) x 51'5", one-and-a-half stories, gable roof, chimney at each gable end and one on each rear slope; five gabled dormers above the recessed porch which extends across the front of the house. Center-hall plan, with four rooms downstairs, two above. Built c. 1857 for William Garrett, whose father, Jacob Garrett, was among the earliest settlers at San Augustine. 4 sheets (1934, including site plan, plans, elevations, sections, details); 5 ext. photos (1934), 1 int. photo (1934); 1 data page (1936).

Hale-Blount House (TEX-240)
3 miles W. of San Augustine on Tex. 21

Wooden frame, two stories, gable roof, chimney at each gable end, pedimented one-story entrance porch at front, shed-roofed one-story lean-to at rear with central recessed porch, gabled addition at left rear, and hip-roofed laundry pavilion at front. Built in 1854 by A. G. Hale, it was the home of Confederate Captain T. W. Blount for more than 60 years. 2 ext. photos (1936); 1 data page (1936). NR.

Sublett, Colonel Philip A., House (TEX-241)
3 miles E. of San Augustine on Tex. 21

Wooden frame, five-bay front, two stories, gable roof, chimney at each gable end, rectangular plan, low hip-roofed entrance porch over broad front door. Built 1860. 1 ext. photo (1936), 1 int. photo (1936); 1 data page (1936).

SAN ELIZARIO
El Paso County (71)

"El Palacio" (See *Viceregal House*)

First El Paso County Courthouse (See *Los Portales*)

Los Portales (First El Paso County Courthouse) (TEX-3107)
San Elizario Plaza

Museum. Adobe and stucco, one story, flat-roofed with long, ten-bay recessed porch facing the plaza. Rectangular plan, with projections enclosing the ends of the porch. Built as a residence, it was donated to San Elizario for use as a school from c. 1885. Although its use as the first El Paso County Courthouse from 1850 has been disputed, it was probably built before that date. Restored 1967. 2 ext. photos (1936); 1 data page (1936).

Lujan, Jesús, House (TEX-3108)
Gone. Formerly adjoining San Elizario Plaza

Adobe, six-bay front, one story, flat-roofed. Built by Jesús Lujan c. 1850. Typical early residence of El Paso area. Roof was of wattle between log joists covered with thatch and mud. 3 ext. photos (1936); 1 data page (1936).

San Elizario Presidio Chapel (TEX-3106)
San Elizario Plaza

Adobe and stucco with bell gable, flat-roofed, three-aisle plan with three semicircular apses. Original construction c. 1783. Interior completely altered by redecorating of 1935 and 1944. 4 ext. photos (1936), 1 int. photo (1936); 2 data pages (1936). NR.

Viceregal House ("El Palacio") (TEX-3110)
2 blocks SE. of San Elizario Plaza

Adobe and stucco, one story, flat roof. Eleven rooms surround three sides of a patio enclosed on the fourth side by a wall. The interiors are noted for the painted tree on the wall of the "throne room." Although indisputably old, this house may not have been erected by Don Juan de Castaneda in 1683. It was acquired in 1968 for restoration by El Paso Landmarks, Inc. 5 ext. photos (1936), 4 int. photos (1936); 2 data pages (1936).

SAN YGNACIO Zapata County (253)

San Ygnacio Ranch Buildings (Treviño House) (TEX-3112) Uribe and Treviño Sts. (Business Route U.S. 83)

Adobe plastered sandstone, 84' x 128', one story, ell-shaped, walled courtyard complex, with rooms along the north and west sides, single slope roofs originally of native concrete or "Chipichil," over wood beams with ornamental brackets. An unusual sundial is above the only exterior entrance to the courtyard on the north facade. The architect and builder was Jesús Treviño and portions of the construction are dated 1851, 1854 and 1871. 5 sheets (1936, including site plan, plans, elevations, section, details) ; 11 ext. photos (1936), 6 int. photos (1936) ; 2 data pages (1936).

San Ygnacio Ranch Buildings, San Ygnacio/Arthur Stewart, Photo 1936

San Ygnacio Ranch Buildings/Arthur Stewart, Photo 1936

SEGUIN   Guadalupe County (94)

Aunt Margaret's House (TEX-348)
Gone

Adobe and river gravel, plastered, one story, one room,
gable roof, chimney at one gable end, lean-to shed attached.
Built in the 1850's and used as a school and post office before
it was deeded to the ex-slave by whose name it was known.
2 ext. photos (1936); 1 data page (1936).

Baxter-Fennell House (Dr. J. D. Fennell House) (TEX-347)
202 E. Walnut St.

Wooden frame and clapboarding, five-bay front, two stories
gable roof, chimney at each gable end. Built by W. C. Baxter
in 1851 and occupied by Fennells since 1860. 4 ext. photos
(1936); 2 data pages (1937).

Campbell, Mosey, House (TEX-329)
Gone.

Concrete, two-and-a-half stories, with gable roof and gabled dormers, galleried veranda on three sides, and recessed attic floor porches under both gable ends. Exterior stair, lean-to kitchen on fourth side. Built 1851. 7 ext. photos (1936), 2 int. photos (1936) ; 1 data page (1936).

Coopender, Luke, House (TEX-344)
Gone.

Concrete, one story, gable roof with central chimney. Built 1850 by Luke Coopender and Dr. Richard Parks, a chemist, who developed a concrete widely used in Seguin residential construction in the 1850's. 3 ext. photos (1936), 1 int. photo (1936) ; 1 data page (1936).

Erskine House #1 (See *Humphrey-Erskine House*)

Erskine House #2 (TEX-343)
513 E. Nolte St.

Log and concrete, four-bay front, one story, gable (later hip) roof. Irregular plan. Built in 1852 with many changes and additions in 1871. 5 ext. photos (1936), 1 int. photo (1936) ; 1 data page (1937).

Fennell, Dr. J. D., House (See *Baxter-Fennell House*)

Flores, Manuel, House (TEX-340)
Gone.

Fieldstone and stucco, five-bay front, two stories including half-basement, hip roof, classical proportions and symmetry. Built 1820-25. 6 ext. photos (1936, including ruins of storehouse and cistern), 1 int. photo (1936) ; 1 data page (1936).

Herron, Parson Andrew, House (TEX-345)
906 W. Court St.

Sandstone ashlar, five-bay front, two stories and cellar, gable roof, two-story front porch, rectangular plan. Interior walnut stair balustrade delicately proportioned. Built 1854 by Parson Andrew Herron, a pioneer Presbyterian minister in Seguin. 4 ext. photos (1936), 1 int. photo (1936) ; 1 data page (1936).

Herron-Vaughn House (Tom Vaughn House) (TEX-346)
S. Goodrich Street

Adobe and gravel with stucco, two stories on slope, only upper story visible from front, gable roofs, 18"-thick walls. L-plan. Built c. 1852 by Parmonia Herron, son of Parson Andrew Herron. 20th-century changes to the front porch conceal the age of the structure, long known as the Vaughn House. 2 ext. photos (1936), 1 int. photo (1936), 1 ext. photo of adjacent kitchen (1936).

Hollamon House (TEX-350)
315 Glen Cove Dr.

Wooden frame with clapboarding and board and concrete, one story, gable roofs, extending over six-post front veranda, irregular plan, originally gable-end chimneys. Two board-and-batten shallow gabled rear ell additions, connected by exposed stair rising from porch to gable-end storeroom. An original log structure of four rooms and center hall, built 1840, was the nucleus of the 1850 construction by Paris Smith, Th. H. and G. B. Hollamon of Virginia, using Dr. Richard Parks' formula for concrete. 5 ext. photos (1936) ; 1 data page (1937).

Humphrey-Erskine House (Erskine House #1) (TEX-328)
902 N. Austin St.

Wooden mortised frame with clapboarding, concrete-filled studding, 18' x 36', two stories, gable roof, two-storied galleried veranda. One- and two-story extensions to the left and rear. Rectangular plan. Built c. 1850. The house attained its present appearance through an early concrete addition to a building moved, in three sections, from Prairie Lea by Dr. D. H. Humphrey in 1867. 4 sheets (1936, including site plan, plans, elevations, details) ; 9 ext. photos (1936), 1 int. photo (1936) ; 1 data page (1937). NR.

Humphrey-Erskine House, Seguin/Arthur Stewart, Photo 1936

Isom's House (TEX-349)
Gone.

Adobe and river gravel, plastered, one story, gable roof extending over rear recessed porch. Built in the early 1850's by Joe Johnson for his slave, Isom. 3 ext. photos (1936); 1 data page (1936).

Johnson-LeGette-Miller House (Thad B. Miller House) (TEX-341)
Johnson Avenue

Concrete and limestone, five-bay front, two stories and cellar, gable roof, two-story entrance porch, rectangular plan. Built by Joseph Johnson of Virginia in 1847 in a residential development he called Guadalupe City. An excellent example of the durability of Dr. Richard Parks' concrete. 9 ext. photos (1936); 2 data pages (1937).

Magnolia Hotel (TEX-327)
203 S. Crockett St.

Wooden frame, two stories, low roof concealed by cornice, T-plan with one-story gabled structure of concrete attached at rear. This portion, built c. 1846, is said to be older than the imposing wooden frame portion which was built by Dr. W. S. Reid. The ballroom was a social center for Seguin, and before the coming of the railroad the hotel was a stagecoach station. 4 ext. photos (1936); 1 data page (1937).

Miller, Thad B., House (See *Johnson-LeGette-Miller House*)

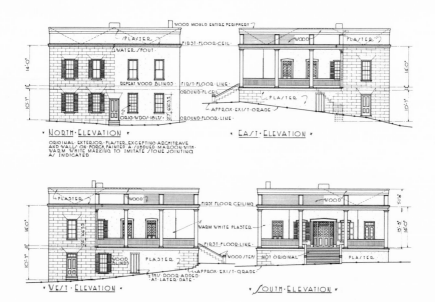

"Sebastopol" (Col. Joshua Young House), Seguin/Bartlett Cocke, Del. 1934

"Sebastopol" (Col. Joshua Young House) (Joseph Zorn House) (TEX-33-A-9)
704 Mill Ave. (W. Court Street)

Museum. Concrete, 46' x 53', one story with basement at the rear, the hip roof is a reservoir concealed by a broad horizontal fascia, a veranda surrounds three sides of the stem of the T-plan. The house was built by Colonel Joshua Young c. 1851 for his daughter, Mrs. Katherine LeGette. It was for many years occupied by the family of Joseph Zorn, who served as mayor and postmaster. Restored by Seguin Conservation Society. 5 sheets (1934, including site plan, plans, elevations, sections and details) ; 5 ext. photos (1934) ; 2 data pages (1936). NR.

Vaughn, Tom, House (See *Herron-Vaughn House*)

White, Judge John P., House (TEX-351)
Gone.

Concrete, one story, gable roof, L-plan, front and rear porches. Built in late 1850's. 4 ext. photos (1936) ; 1 data page (1936).

Young, Colonel Joshua, House (See *"Sebastopol"*)

Zorn, Joseph, House (See *"Sebastopol"*)

SHAFTER VICINITY

Presidio County (189)

Fortin de Cibolo (Little Fort of Cibolo) (TEX-3118)
Cibolo Creek, about 4 miles NW. of Shafter on J. E. White and Sons ranch

Adobe block, originally 100' square with circular defense towers at the north and south corners, one story, flat-roofed with adobe over a platform of cottonwood saplings. Heavy, paneled doors, wood-grilled windows. A private fort, designed for protection against Indian attack, was built in the 1850's by Milton Faver on his sheep range, between a hill on the east and Cibolo Creek on the west. 8 ext. photos (1936) ; 2 data pages (1937).

Fortin de Cienega (Little Fort of Cienega) (TEX-3119)
Near source of Cienega Creek, about 6 miles E. of Shafter,
on the Hart Greenwood Ranch

Adobe block, 89'7" square including stockade with square defense towers at the northeast and southwest, with living quarters in 13'-wide rooms along the south and west perimeter; one story, flat-roofed. Originally there was no exit or entrance except via the main gate. Built in the late 1850's by Milton Faver, it was on one of several of his Mexican Longhorn cattle ranges. 3 sheets (1936, including site plan, plans, elevations, sections, details) ; 1 ext. photo (1936) ; 2 data pages (1937).

SNYDER VICINITY   Scurry County (208)

Harrell House (See LUBBOCK, Lubbock County)

NORTH ELEVATION

SOUTH ELEVATION

Harrell House, Snyder Vicinity (moved to Lubbock)/
Elizabeth Sasser, Del. 1973

El Paso County (71)

Mission Nuestra Señora del Socorro, Church (TEX-3105)
Moon Road at Farm Road 258

Adobe, thick-walled and stuccoed, 72′ x 122′5″; flat roof supported by carved beams bearing on corbels, stepped parapet of facade rises into a single-bell campanario. H-plan. Socorro, settled by refugees from the 1680 pueblo uprising in New Mexico, claims to be the oldest continuous settlement in Texas, although it was an 1840 flood which changed the course of the Rio Grande to take it from the Mexican side. This flood washed away the old church which was reconstructed at a new site using the ceiling beams from the 18th-century structure. Although not completed until 1848, this mission church is more historically authentic in its design than other El Paso area examples on the Texas side of the river. 7 sheets (1936, including site plan, plans, elevations, section, details) ; 6 ext. photos (1936), 3 int. photos (1936) ; 4 data pages (1936). NR.

Mission Nuestra Señora del Socorro, Socorro/Marvin Eichenroht, Photo 1936

SOMERSET VICINITY

Cowan, I. M., House (TEX-382)
Gone.

Stone and stucco, four-bay front, one story, gable roof,
rectangular plan with lean-tos front and rear. Built 1858. 3
ext. photos (1936); 1 data page (1936).

STONEHAM VICINITY

Sanders-McIntyre House (TEX-224)
Gone.

Log, one story, gable roof extended over recessed front
porch, stone chimney at one gable end. Built by K. P. Sanders
in 1826 for Margaret McIntyre and her two sons who had
come from Ireland to Texas among the Austin colonists. 1
ext. photo (1936); 1 data page (1936).

"Whitehall" (Colonel Joseph H. Polley House), Sutherland Springs
Vicinity/W. Cook, Del. 1936

SUTHERLAND SPRINGS VICINITY
Wilson County (247)

"Whitehall" (Colonel Joseph H. Polley House) (TEX-326)
3 miles N. on Farm Road 539

Local stone, coursed rubble, 53'3" (five-bay front) x 46'3",
two stories, gable roof, two-story porch across front. Center-
hall plan. "Whitehall" also includes a separate log kitchen,
15' square, with stone fireplace and chimney, and, as shown
in photos, a stone cistern. Built between 1848 and 1854 by
Joseph H. Polley, a native of New York, who came to Texas
as one of the Austin colonists. 7 sheets (1936, including site
plan, plans, elevations, section, details) ; 6 ext. photos (1936),
1 ext. photo kitchen (1936), 1 ext. photo log cabin (1936) ;
2 data pages (1936).

TAYLOR VICINITY
Williamson County (246)

McFadin, D. H., House (TEX-339)
5 miles NE. on Farm Road 1331, 1 mile E. of Tex. 95

Limestone and stucco, two stories, rectangular plan with
two-story entrance porch. Built between 1840 and 1850 for
D. H. McFadin, a wealthy rancher. 3 ext. photos (1936) ; 1
data page (1937.)

THOMASTON VICINITY
De Witt County (62)

Murphree, Thomas, House (TEX-279)
Gone.

Limestone and wooden frame with clapboarding, one story
with raised basement, gable roof, chimney at one gable end,
rectangular plan; five-bay, two-level porch across front, ornamental upper deck spandrels. Principal rooms in wooden
frame upper section, service rooms in stone basement. Built
1848 as the center of a large cattle ranch. 1 ext. photo
(1936) ; 1 data page (1936).

Thomas Murphree House, Thomaston Vicinity/Harry L. Starnes, Photo 1936

TRUSCOTT VICINITY
King County (135)

Masterson Rock Bunkhouse (See LUBBOCK, Lubbock County)

VICTORIA
Victoria County (235)

Callender, William L., House (TEX-247)
404 W. Guadalupe St.

Wooden frame, 44'3" (five-bay front) x 55'3", two stories and raised basement, gable roof, pitch extends over giant portico, with five shallow arches cut into the wooden fascia marking the bays between six square-sided columns. Flight of steps leads to porch deck and main floor. Half-frame windows in second story slide into the wall horizontally when opened. Precut lumber was ordered from the east by Dr. Stephen F. Cocke in 1854, the house built in 1855. Occupied from 1871 to 1895 by William L. Callender, an attorney whose family added a rear two-story wing. 4 sheets

(1936, including plans, elevations, section, details) ; 1 ext.
photo (1936) ; 1 data page (1936).

Goldman, A., House (TEX-245)
Gone.

Wooden frame, one story, gable roof, L-plan, with six-
column porch across front. Built 1866. 1 ext. photo (1936) ;
1 data page (1936).

Rupley Building (TEX-280)
Gone

Brick, two stories, gable roof, ornamental iron porches.
Built 1859-60. 1 ext. photo (1936) ; 1 data page (1936).

WASHINGTON AND VICINITY
Washington County (239)

"Barrington" (Anson Jones House) (TEX-212)
Washington-on-the-Brazos State Park

Museum. Wooden frame, one story, gable roof with two
chimneys at each gable end, porch across front, rectangular
and center hall plans. Built 1844 for Dr. Anson Jones, Secretary of State, Minister to the United States, and President of
the Republic of Texas at the time of annexation to the United
States. Moved and restored since 1936. 3 ext. photos (1936) ;
1 data page (1936).

Brown, John M., House (TEX-213)
SW. of Washington, 1.5 miles on Farm Road 912

Wooden frame, 53'10" (five-bay front) x 35'11", two stories,
low hip roof, rectangular plan, one-story Doric porches,
front and rear, elegant in proportions and detailing. Shuttered floor-to-ceiling windows both stories. Center-hall plan
with graceful stair curving at upper end. Built 1855. Finish
materials and mouldings are said to have been shipped from
New York via Galveston. Architect, John Watson. The original owner, John M. Brown, was a planter from South
Carolina. Restored. 5 sheets (1936, including site plan, plans,
elevations, sections, details) ; 2 ext. photos (1936), 1 int.
photo (1936) ; 1 data page (1936).

Jones, Anson, House (See *"Barrington"*)

WEBBERVILLE VICINITY   Bastrop County (11)

Burleson, Aaron, House (TEX-3126)
Gone.

Brick, one story, gable roof, linear plan, four rooms, each with fireplace, shed-roofed porch extended full length of one side; high, ornamental brick cornice. Built by a Colonel Banks in early 1860's. 4 ext. photos (1937), 1 int. photo of mantel (1937); 1 data page (1937).

Ireland, Tom, House (TEX-337)
Gone.

Log, one story, gable roof, dog-trot cabin. Built in 1840's. 3 ext. photos (1937); 1 data page (1937).

Varner-Hogg Plantation House, West Columbia Vicinity/
Harry L. Starnes, Photo 1936

WEST COLUMBIA VICINITY   Brazoria County (20)

Varner-Hogg Plantation House (TEX-251)
2 miles N. of West Columbia at Varner-Hogg State Park

Museum. Brick and stucco, five-bay front, two stories, gable roof with square cupola, rectangular plan, two-story veranda front and rear. Kitchen-dining room in adjacent building. Built c. 1835 by Columbus R. Patton, who may have enclosed the cabin of Martin Varner, original owner of the plantation. Purchased in 1901 by James Stephen Hogg, Governor of Texas (1891-95), whose family adapted it to new needs by extension remodeling. 4 ext. photos (1936); 1 data page (1936); HABSI.

YSLETA   El Paso County (71)

Mission Nuestra Señora del Carmen (Mission Corpus Christi de la Isleta del Sur) (TEX-3104)
U.S. 80 at Farm Road 258 (Alameda Avenue at Old Pueblo Drive)

Adobe and stucco, corner tower, flat roof, Latin cross plan. Elements of the building date from 1683. The floods of 1840 shifted the river bed and left the building on the east bank, which was ultimately to be inside the boundary of Texas. The interior and tower of Mission Isleta were almost totally destroyed by fire in 1906. With the final rebuilding an effort was made to reproduce the appearance of the old church, but since the work was done under the care of the Mission Señora del Carmen, that name was subsequently adopted. 5 ext. photos (1936), 2 int. photos (1936); 2 data pages (1936). NR.

ZAPATA VICINITY   Zapata County (253)

San Bartolo Ranch Buildings (TEX-3113)
Gone.

Sandstone, flat and gable roofs, one story; flat roofs of native concrete or "chipichil." A total of eight buildings were built in this complex between 1867 and 1876 under the direction of Luis Gutierres. Rafter inscriptions confirmed the dates. Site submerged by Falcon Reservoir. 5 ext. photos (1936); 2 data pages (1936).

San Bartolo Ranch Buildings, Zapata Vicinity/Arthur Stewart, Photo 1936

HABS TEXAS INVENTORY LIST (HABSI)

NOTE: This list includes structures recorded solely on HABS Inventory forms. Structures which have also been more fully recorded by HABS are listed only in the catalog.

Town	*County*	*Building*
Albany	Shackelford	Fort Griffin
Bastrop	Bastrop	Bastrop Christian Church
Bevilport	Jasper	Smyth, Captain Andrew Forney, House
Brownsville	Cameron	Stillman House
Buffalo Gap	Taylor	Old Taylor County Court House and Jail
Columbus	Colorado	Colorado County Court House
Corpus Christi	Nueces	Old Bernard Place
		Centennial House (Evans House)
		St. Patrick's Cathedral
Dallas	Dallas	First Baptist Church
		Bryan, John Neely, Cabin
		Hord, Judge W. H., House
		Millermore
Decatur	Wise	Waggoner Ranch House
El Paso	El Paso	Mexican Consulate
Galveston	Galveston	The Adak Building
		2115 Strand
		Adoue-Lobit Bank
		2102 Strand
		Aiken-McGlathery House
		1312 Sealy
		Aiken-Opperman House
		1316 Sealy
		Ansell, Walter C., House
		3702 Avenue M
		Block, Louis, House
		1804 Ball
		Blum, Leon and H., Building
		2310-2328 Mechanic
		B'nai Israel Synagogue
		707 22nd St.
		Brock, Anthony, House
		3410 Avenue L

Brown, J. S., Building
2111 Strand
Brown, J. S., Hardware Co. Building
2226-2228 Strand
Brush Electric Light & Power Co.
Building
SW. corner 26th and Postoffice
Carnes, Howard, House
1914 Avenue M
Chase, Frederick W., House
1412 Market
Clarke, Charles, House
1728 Sealy
Clarke and Courts Building
2406 Mechanic
Colleraine, Edward A., House
612 17th St.
Darragh, J. L., House
1827 Church
Davis, Jake, House
1802 Postoffice
Davis, Waters S., Sr., House
1124 28th St.
Dealy, Thomas W., House
1217 Church
Engine House No. 5
1614 Avenue K
Everett, Alexander B., House
1211 Church
Fadden, James, Building
2410-2412 Strand
First Evangelical Lutheran Church
SW. corner 24th and Winnie
First National Bank Building
2127 Strand
Focke, Wilkens & Lange Building
2301-2311 Strand
Foster, James W., House
3523 Avenue P
Fox, C. G., Building
2024-2028 Mechanic
Galveston Bagging & Cordage Co.

Warehouse
Winnie between 39th and 40th
Galveston Cotton and Woolen Mills
Winnie between 40th and 41st
Galveston Water and Electric Light
Station
NW. corner 30th and Ball
Garrett House
3517 Avenue M
Gengler, Peter, House
1426 Market
Goggans, Thomas, House
1804 Church
Grace Episcopal Church
1115 36th St.
Grand Opera House and Hotel Grand
2012-2020 Postoffice
Greenleve, Block & Company Building
2314 Strand
Hagemann, John, House
3301 Avenue L
Hartley House
1121 33rd St.
The Heidenheimer Building
2127 Mechanic
Heidenheimer Building
303 21st St.
Heidenheimer's Building, Addition
2109 Mechanic
Heye, Gustave, House
1226 Postoffice
House
1510 Church
Hurley, Charles, House
1328 Ball
Hutchings, Sealy & Co. Building
2326-2328 Strand
Jackson, James, House
1803 Postoffice
Johnson, McKenzie, House
1916 Avenue K
Kauffman and Runge Building

222 22nd St.
Kruger, Rudolph E., House
1626-1628 Postoffice
Lammers, Francis, House
1118 Market
Lang, Mrs., Building
2109 Strand
Langbehn, J. Henry, House
1102 Sealy
Lasker Home for Homeless Children
(McLemore House)
1019 16th St.
League, John Charles, House
1710 Broadway
Magale, J. F., Building
2313-2315 Strand
Mallory Building
2114 Strand
Marschner, C. F., Building
1914-1916 Mechanic
Mason, George, House
1624 Postoffice
Masonic Temple (Old)
2027 Postoffice
Meininger, William, Residence
1722 Church
Merchants Mutual Insurance Co.
Building
2313-2319 Strand
Meyer, Mrs. Emma, House
1717-1719 Church
Meyer, Gustave A., House
1202 21st St.
Meyer, Gustave A., Building
2015 Market
Minor, Lucian, House
2217-2219 Avenue H
Moller, Jens, House
1814 Sealy
Moody, W. L., Building
2202-2206 Strand
Moore, Stratton & Company Building

2120-2128 Strand
Moser, Mrs. E., House
1827 Postoffice
Muller, Frederick William, House
1713-1715 Winnie
Painter, Harry A., House
1204 37th St.
Peacock House
1620 Postoffice
Pechanec House
1112 Postoffice
Reedy Memorial Chapel
2013 Broadway
Reymershoffer, Gus, House
1302 Postoffice
Rice, Baulard and Company Building
200 block Tremont
Roensch, Bernard, House
1517 Ball
Rosenberg Building
2309-2311 Strand
Rosenberg's Building
2005-2011 Strand
Rosenberg, Letitia, Women's Home
1804 Rosenberg
Ruhl, Julius, House
1428 Sealy
Sacred Heart Catholic Church
1400 Broadway
St. Patrick's Catholic Church
NW. corner 34th and K
Sampson, Arthur F., House
1720 Postoffice
Sawyer, William D., House
1822-1824 Church
Schneider, George, House
1208 Ball
Schneider, George, & Co. Building
2101 Strand
Schott, Justus J., House
1507 Market
Scott, J. Z. H., House

1721 Broadway
Scrimgeour, Capt. William, House
   810 Postoffice
Smith, J. F., and Brothers Building
   2321-2323 Strand
Smith, John F., House
   2217 Broadway
Smith, R. Waverly, House
   3017 Avenue O
Sonnentheil, Jacob, House
   1822-1826 Sealy
Star Drug Store
   510 Tremont
Sweeney, Thomas S., House
   2402 Avenue L
Tartt, Boling G., Building
   SE. corner Tremont and Winnie
Texas Star Flour Mills and Elevator
   2010-2028 Water
Thompson, Dr. Thomas C., House
   1503 Sealy
Tiernan, Barney, House
   1501 Market
Wallis, Landes & Company Building
   2411 Strand
West, Dr. Hamilton A., House
   1202 Ball
Willis, P. J., & Bros. Building
   100 block 24th St.
Willis, Richard M., House
   2618 Broadway

Gruene	Comal	Western Texas Orphan Asylum
Hawley	Jones	Fort Phantom Hill
Houston	Harris	St. Peter Evangelical Lutheran Church
		San Felipe Cottage
Laredo	Webb	Casa Ortiz
		San Augustine Church
Llano	Llano	The Southern Hotel
New Braunfels	Comal	Breustedt, Andreas, House
		Tietze, F. W., House
Oakville	Live Oak	Old Live Oak County Jail

Refugio	Refugio	Heard House
Rockport	Aransas	Balthrope House
		Bruhl House
San Antonio	Bexar	"Acosta" House

"Acosta" House
138 Goliad
Aldrete House
326 E. Nueva St.
"Amaya" House
201 Wyoming
"Arciniega" House
220 Arciniega St.
Beckmann, Albert F., House
529 Madison St.
Beisenbach, August, House
528 King William St.
Blersch, Gustave, House
213 Washington St.
Bombach House (The Little Rhein)
231 South Alamo
Brackenridge, George W., House
4515 Broadway
Chabot, George S., House
403 Madison
Devine, Daniel, Building
112 East Main Plaza
Devine, Gregory P., Building
108 East Main Plaza
Diaz House
206 Arciniega
Dugosh, Albert, House
414 Matagorda
Dugosh, Albert, House (Coyone
House, Tynan House)
405 Goliad
Dullnig Building
101 Alamo Plaza
Dullnig, George W., Houses
515 Elm, 122 Nolan, 204 Nolan
Eagar, Robert, House and Dependency
434 South Alamo
Edmunds, Colonel Elias, House
419 King William St.

Ellis, Smith M., House (Ike West
    House)
    422 King William St.
"Espinoza" House
    533 Water
Faville, Franklin D., House (Florian
    House)
    510 Villita
Froebel, Martin, House
    228 Washington St.
German-English School
    419 South Alamo
German Methodist Episcopal Church
    ("Little Church of La Villita")
    508 La Villita
Gissi, Cirulus, House
    141 South St.
Gressner, Louis, House
    225 South Presa St.
Groos, Carl Wilhelm August, House
    (Martha Manor)
    335 King William St.
Groos, Gustav, House
    231 Washington St.
Guenther, Carl H., House
    205 Guenther St.
Halff, Meyer, House
    139 N. Goliad
Halff, Solomon, House
    142 Goliad St.
Hanschke, Robert, House
    225 King William St.
Harnisch, Carl, House
    523 King William St.
House
    933 North Flores St.
House
    325 South Presa St.
Hummel, Charles F. A., House
    309 King William St.
Joske, Alexander, House
    245 King William St.

Joseph, Adam, House
409 Avenue E
"Koehler" House
527 Water St.
Kusch, John, House
301 Goliad
Lang, George W., House (Dan
Sullivan House)
404 Broadway
Lieber House
412 South Presa St.
Martin, J. F., House (Juliana C. Van
Derlip House)
337 Madison St.
Pereida, R. M., House
502 South Alamo
Phillip, Anton, House (Staffel House)
422 South Presa St.
"Quinta Urrutia"
3200 block of Broadway
Ramsay & Ford Building (St. Paul's
Bookstore)
114 E. Main Plaza
Richter, C. A., House
401 Goliad St.
San Antonio City Hall
Military Square
San Antonio National Bank Building
(First National Bank of San
Antonio)
213 W. Commerce St.
Sartor, Alex, House
217 King William St.
Schultze, Hermann, House
HemisFair Plaza
Schultze, Maximilian, House
331 Goliad
Schultze Store & Hardware Co.
Building
HemisFair Plaza
Smith, Deaf, House
301 South Presa St.

Smith, Sam, House
503 Water St.
Southern Manufacturing Co. Building
216 South Flores St.
Stevens, John James, House
303 King William St.
Steves, Edward, Jr., House
431 King William St.
St. Joseph's Church
221 E. Commerce
Sweeney, James, House
117 Goliad
Sweet, James R., House
4515 Broadway
Thiele House
411 Sixth St.
Thiele House
415 Sixth St.
Tynan, Walter C., House
401 South Presa St.
Wietzel, Jacob, House
135 Wyoming
Wolfson, L., Store
415 W. Commerce
Wurzbach, Charles Lewis, House
419 8th St.
Wurzbach, Charles Lewis, House (Uhl
House)
407 8th St.
Yturri House
440 East Commerce
Yturri, Manuel, House
327 South Presa St.
Yturri-Edmunds House
257 Yellowstone St.

Victoria	Victoria	Sibley Building
Waxahachie	Ellis	Ellis County Courthouse
Weatherford	Parker	Parker County Courthouse

INDEX

63769